A Hannes Bok Showcase

EDITED BY STEPHEN D. KORSHAK

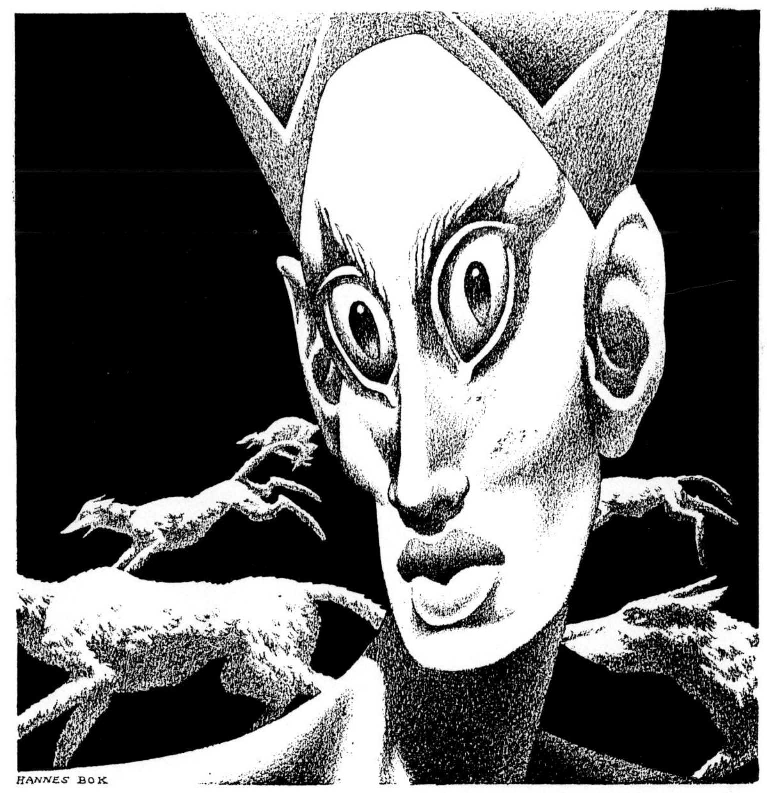

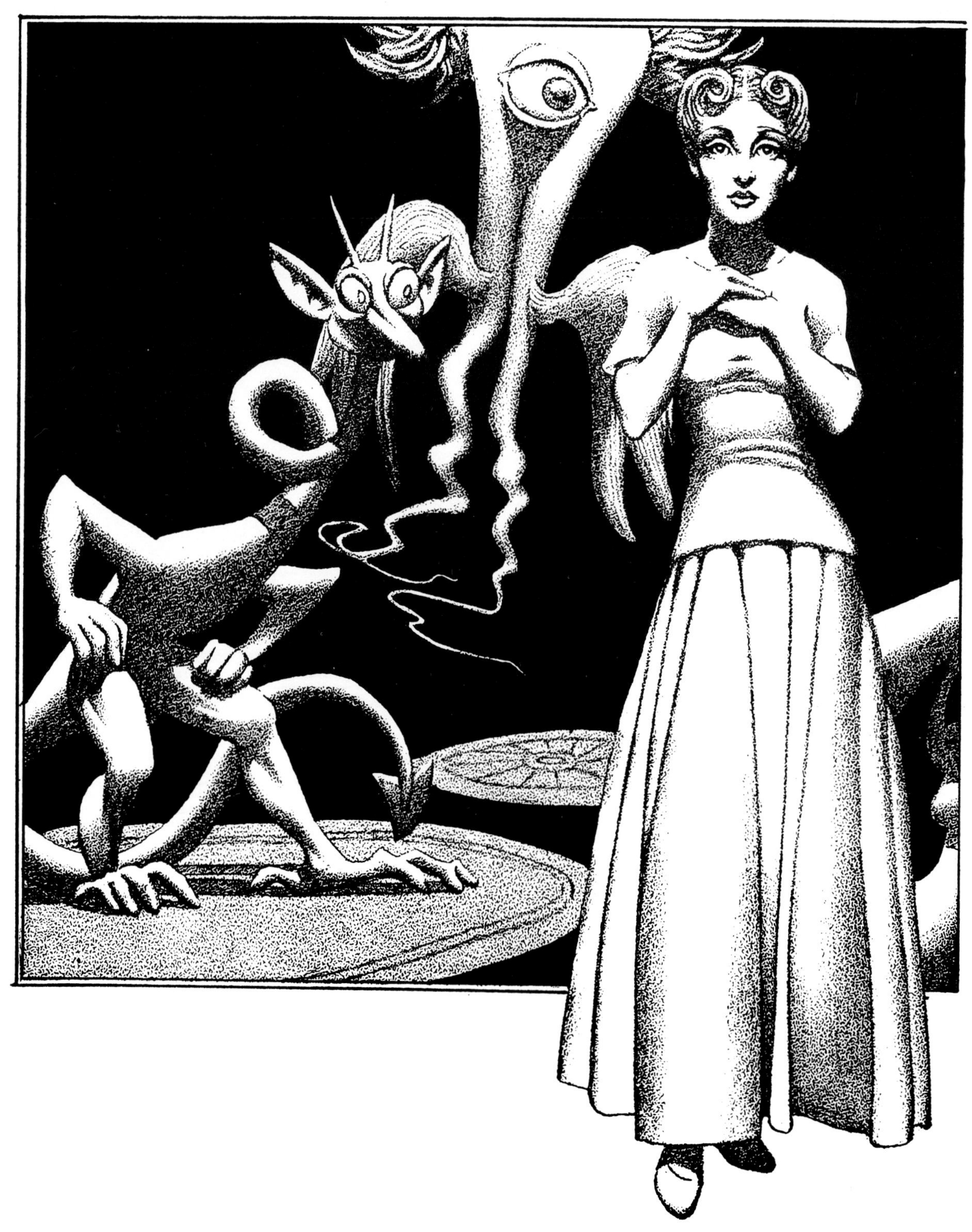

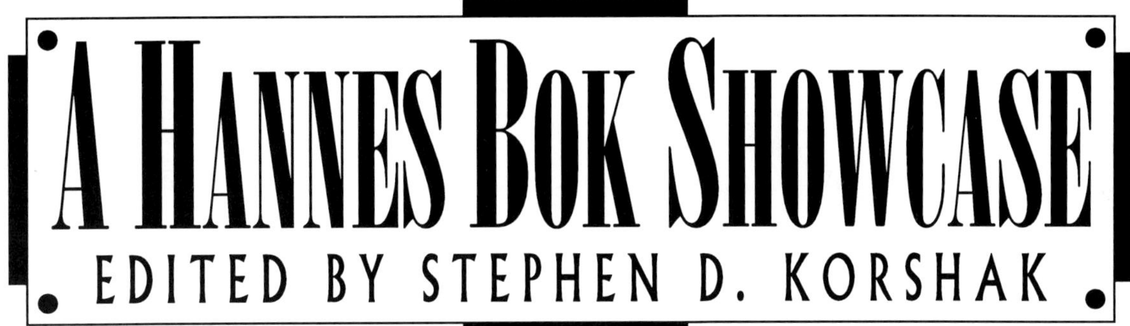

A HANNES BOK SHOWCASE
EDITED BY STEPHEN D. KORSHAK

Foreword by
Frederik Pohl

CHARLES F. MILLER
PUBLISHER
Lancaster, Pennsylvania

A Hannes Bok Showcase
ISBN 1-885611-06-4 (softcover edition)
ISBN 1-885611-05-6 (hardcover edition)

Book Design: Charles F. Miller

A third collection of Hannes Bok's artwork is being readied for publication. Anyone with information about original Bok artwork should contact the editor: Stephen D. Korshak, 2345 Sand Lake Road, Suite 120, Orlando, FL 32809.

Special thanks are due to the following for permission to reproduce in the present volume Bok artwork from their collection: RAH Hoffman, Richard Kelly, Worlds of Wonder, Tom Horvitz, R. F. Wald, Sig Wahrman, Robert Weinberg and Helen and Gerry de la Ree.

*In loving memory
of my Mother*

IRENE KORSHAK

*A friend of Hannes Bok
and a constant inspiration
in my life.*

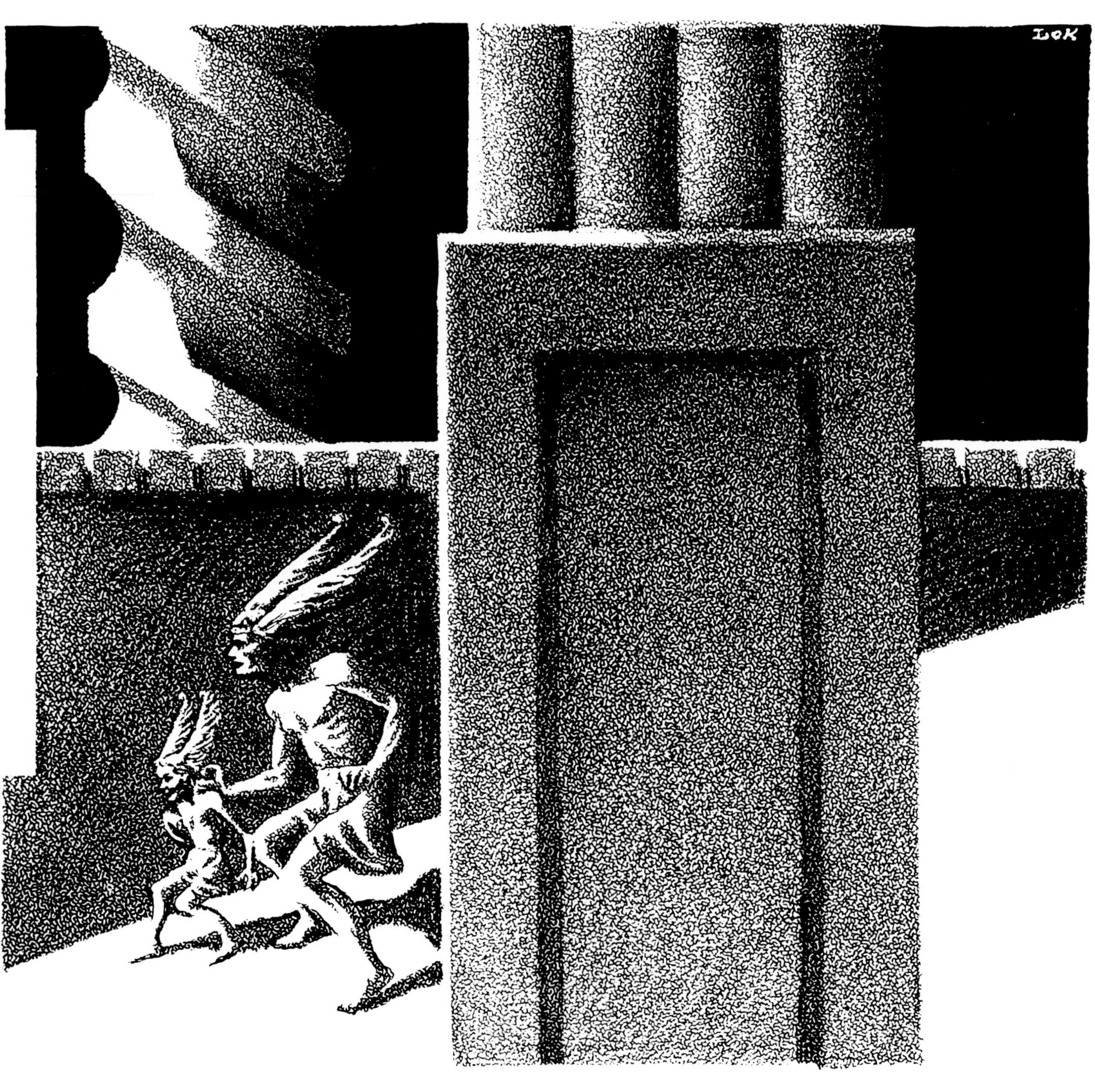

Illustration for "It's a Young World" by Frederik Pohl (as by James MacCreigh).

<u>*REMEMBERING HANNES*</u>

by Frederik Pohl

Framed on a wall of my office is a small black-and-white drawing which shows a willowy man and an equally willowy child. Neither of them looks exactly human, and each is wearing a sort of curious winged helmet as they run through some sort of pillared chamber. It is a beautiful piece of work.

Like most writers, I do have the originals of a couple of magazine and book covers hanging here and there in my house, but this is the only interior illustration I've hung. I cherish it—not only because it comes from one of my earliest published stories, but because the artist who drew it for its magazine appearance was Hannes Bok.

I first met Hannes in the early fall of 1939. It was a propitious time, since an event of inconceivable magnitude had just taken place in my life.

To be sure, everybody's life was filled with astonishing developments at that moment: World War II had just broken out in Europe. In this country the Great Depression was at last beginning to loosen its ten-year grip on the hopes and well-being of Americans. In my home town of New York a great World's Fair had just run its season and showed several million visitors that the World of Tomorrow could be filled with grace and light, and the local fans had seized on the opportunity to put on the first-ever World Science Fiction Convention. All this was interesting enough, of course; but the event that changed everything for me was more personal. I had just achieved my heart's desire.

My heart's desire was handed to me by a man named Harry Steeger. He was the president of Popular Publications, Inc., one of the largest pulp-magazine publishers in the world, and—fortunately for me—he was a reasonably kind man as well. He proved that by spending half an hour patiently listening to my explanation of why it would be a good idea for him to bring out a couple of new magazines in the rapidly growing science fiction field and—oh, yes—since he would probably want to have someone who knew something about the field to handle them, he might as well go ahead and put me on the payroll to be their editor.

And at the end of that half hour, while I was still making my case, he stood up, cutting me short. "Sounds worth trying, Fred," he said. "We'll give it a whirl. You can start work tomorrow."

I have seldom known purer joy than the rapture I felt as I floated home that evening. I had achieved every fan's dream. I was the first kid on my block to have attained the status of full-fledged P*R*O*F*E*S*S*I*O*N*A*L E*D*I*T*O*R and thus, at the unripe age of nineteen, had joined the pantheon of demigods like John Campbell and Hugo Gernsback and F. Orlin Tremaine.

The rapture lasted all that night. It survived the subway trip to East 42d Street the next morning, and was if anything intensified when Steeger carried my own personal typewriter into my very own personal office. It was only afterward that reality began to strike home.

Although Harry Steeger was a reasonably kind man, he wasn't entirely out of his mind. If he committed himself to a gamble on an untried editor in a risky and still tiny publishing field he'd never ventured into before, at least he proposed to keep the stakes low. "We can't give you a very big budget," he told me. "For your first magazine—what did you say you wanted to call it, *Astonishing Stories*? Whatever. Anyway, you'll have to buy stories and features; and of course you'll need art, too."

"Of course I will," I said, swallowing. That part hadn't occurred to me before.

Steeger looked at me curiously, and then went on. "Say thirty dollars for a full-color cover? And another fifty or sixty for inside black-and-white line cuts to illustrate the stories? Let's call it, um, I make it four hundred and five dollars an issue, total. Think you can put it together for that? Sure you can. Good luck."

And then he left me to begin doing arithmetic.

It was my first experience with any kind of budget, because although I had put out a mort of mimeographed magazines in my fannish career I had never had to *pay* for contributions before. I didn't expect fiction to be a problem. I calculated that I could probably buy all the stories I needed for half a cent a word or so. Of course, I wouldn't be able to compete for them with Campbell's *Astounding* or Mort Weisinger's *Thrilling Wonder* with their lavish penny-a-word minimum. On the other hand, they certainly wouldn't buy *everything* that might appear on the market. I was confident I could glean a few decent pieces from among their rejects...and, besides, I had a largely untapped resource that I could mine for stories. I had fandom.

I was a founding member of the New York fan club called the Futurians, and I knew my colleagues. Then as now, the science fiction fan is the larval stage of the science fiction writer. True, not every fan ever manages to pupate and spread his wings in professional print; but the Futurian wannabes were richer in talent than most, and even more determined to make it as pros. We had people like Cyril Kornbluth and Isaac

Asimov, Dirk Wylie and Robert Lowndes, Don Wollheim and Dick Wilson—a little later, Damon Knight and James Blish. Some of us had already begun to sell a piece to the prozines now and then, and we were all *ready*.

So stories were not really a problem...but what about this "art" stuff that Harry Steeger wanted me to buy? Where was I to go for that?

I scratched around—among the regular Popular Pubs artists (most of them wouldn't dream of working for the pitiful money I had to pay them, but the Popular art director, Aleck Portegal, whipped a few into line for me); among my girlfriend's fellow art students at Cooper Union; among the fans themselves. And then I struck gold. A West Coast fan named Hannes Bok showed up at a Futurian meeting.

• • •

Hanne's arrival was not entirely unanticipated, because a few weeks earlier a Californian named Ray Bradbury, a nineteen-year-old like myself, had taken the long bus ride from Los Angeles to New York. Ray's main purpose was to attend the first-ever World Science Fiction Convention, but he had two other objectives in mind. One was to get to cozy up to some editors, in the hopes that one or two of them might finally break down and buy some of the short stories he'd been unsuccessfully trying to get them to print. The other was to persuade those same editors to hire his Seattle artist-fan-friend, Hannes Bok, to illustrate some of their magazines. Ray had brought samples of Hanne's work to show around; and then, just when my need was greatest, Hannes followed up in person.

In 1939 Hannes Bok was all of twenty-five years old and thus a senior citizen among us, but he looked younger. He looked—well, "elfin" is the word that others have used to describe him, and it does as well as any. It wasn't just a matter of his physical appearance. His manner was both reserved and, well, flighty, not to say downright evasive; there were obviously huge hunks of Hannes's internal life which he did not care to share even with his friends. Although he read a lot of science fiction and was thrilled at the chance to illustrate it, he had substantial interests elsewhere. We got an inkling of what some of them involved when, startling us all, he offered to cast a horoscope for any Futurian who wished it done. That took us aback. We pragmatically hard-nosed science fiction types were perfectly willing to believe in Martians and time travel, but astrology was way outside the limits of our tolerance.

But we were willing to put up with almost anything from Hannes. He was a good friend to have...and most of all, he won us with his talent. The man drew like an angel.

Well, not entirely like an angel; I don't believe that angels ever sweat. Hannes did. He worked harder at his drawings and paintings than anyone else I knew. At that time, in a rule apparently ordained by God (and only revised decades later), every science fiction and fantasy magazine in America was printed on coarse groundwood pulp paper. The reason for using pulp paper was that it was cheap. The problem with using it was that its thirsty pores caused the ink to smear. This wasn't a significant drawback as far as the text was concerned, because the impressions left by the hot-metal type were not greatly affected. The art was another question. Apart from the covers (which were always printed in full color on coated paper, because they were the billboards that sold the magazines), the illustrations had to be line drawings. The photo-engraving process recognized only two shades. One was white. The other was black. There was nothing in between.

This meant that pencil sketches, for example, were indecipherable for the plate-making cameras; nor could the artist use wash or grays of any kind. For an artist like Hannes, one of whose greatest strengths was in the variety of textures he gave his drawings, that required him to labor endlessly at stippling in little dots of black ink to make the in-between shades.

An artist didn't necessarily *have* to do it that way, of course. The graphics-art technology of the time had produced cellophane-like sheets of overlays (called "Ben-Day") in various patterns and densities which the artist could scissor into whatever shape he wanted to shade. At least, some artists could. That resource, however, was denied to the unfortunates who were trying to make a living by illustrating for publications like my own, for the Ben-Day transparencies cost about as much per square inch as the artists were going to get for the finished illustrations.

So Hannes bent over his drawing board hour after hour, stippling away. I loved his pebbly textures and his wraith-thin human (or were they really human?) figures. Cover paintings, because they were believed to sell the book, required a *nihil obstat* from the publisher, and I was never able to get one of Hannes's covers approved. Still, I used his black and white work as much as I could, especially for the stories I cared about most. (For instance, the ones I had written myself—the drawing that hangs now in my office was originally made for my early novelette, "It's a Young World!" appears on page vi of this volume.) So did my Futurian colleagues, Bob Lowndes and Don Wollheim, when they followed my example and acquired professional science fiction magazines of their own to edit. So, finally, did some of the other science fiction magazines. Farnsworth Wright, editor of *Weird Tales*, had been hospitable to Hannes's work from the very beginning; when Mary Gnaedinger became editor of that other early fantasy magazine, *Famous Fantastic Mysteries*, she used him too; and when the first semi-pro publishers began bringing out actual hardbound science fiction and fantasy books, Hannes did a number of their covers.

But by then I'd almost lost touch with Hannes. There was a war on. I signed up and went off to Italy in the Air Force, and it was a while after the war was over before I had a chance to pick up old friendships again. As far as I can remember, I saw Hannes only once after 1943.

It was not a happy occasion.

• • •

Although even the rates for artists had gone up some since 1939, so had the price of everything else. Hannes had managed to broaden his career by turning to writing, and some of his fantasy novels had been published, but the market for them was not overly well-paid, either; and the last time I saw Hannes, sometime in the late 1950s, he was not doing well. He was living in a furnished room in a run-down neighborhood of uptown Manhattan. He didn't go out much. It wasn't simply that he had become something fairly near a hermit, although he had; it was even more that he didn't have the price of subway fare to waste. He wasn't glowing with health, either. Hannes had lost most of his teeth early, and now he had somehow broken his dentures; he couldn't chew, couldn't eat anything that required chewing, was doing poorly on what soft stuff he could handle. Worse than that, he was self-conscious about it all and not particularly cordial. Nor did we seem to have all that much in common any more. Hannes had pretty much lost interest in science fiction and even in fantasy, as most of us understood it: he was deep into mystic studies, of which astrology was only the least bizarre and incomprehensible to me.

I never saw him again. He lived on for almost another decade, but his buoyancy never returned; and then, in 1963, he died alone in his apartment. His death wasn't even noticed for days.

For a man who spent so much of his life producing pretty things for the rest of us to enjoy, the last stages of Hannes's life, and especially his death, were lacking in prettiness of any kind. He deserved better. His work gave a lot of us a good deal of pleasure, and still goes on doing so for people who weren't even born when he was at his peak.

The work survives; but I do wish Hannes had been able to keep a little more of that pleasure for himself.

FREDERIK POHL

CHRONOLOGY

1914   July 2nd. Born Wayne Woodard in Kansas City, Missouri

1927   Bok reads 3rd installment of *Amazing Stories* with A. Merritt story (July, 1927), "The Moon Pool"

1932   Graduate of Duluth (Minn.) High—Departs for Seattle

1934   (December, 1934—January, 1935) Fantasy Magazine, first appearance of Hannes Bok, publication of linoleum block cover to *Cosmos*, a 17-part science-fiction story signed "Bok"

1936   Publication of artwork for Petaja's BRIEF CANDLE

1937   (or 1938) Moves to Los Angeles

1938   Works on fanzine art for Bradbury's *Futuria Fantasia*

1938   Returns to Seattle—paints "Ase on the Hillock"

1939   First professional cover for *Weird Tales*—"Hannes Bok" born. Moves to New York City, 116 West 109th Street (December, 1939)

1942   Publication of first story "Alien Vibration"—in *Future Fiction*. Publication of Novel "Starstone World"—1942 in *Science-Fiction Quarterly*. Publication of "The Sorcerers Ship" Dec. 1942 in *Unknown Worlds*.

1945   Lithographs "The Power Series"

1945   January 2 through January 13 one-man exhibition at Ferragil Art Gallery, New York

1946   Illustrates and completes the unfinished novels "THE FOX WOMAN" and 'THE BLACK WHEEL" of A. Merritt—paints "Skull-Face"

1948   Publication of "The Blue Flamingo" in January, 1948, *Startling Stories* (appeared in late 1947)

1948   Paints "Slaves of Sleep"

1949   Bok attends his first and only World Science-Fiction Convention, Cincinnati (September 3-5)

1950   Draws "Pickman's Model"

1953   Presented the first Hugo as Best Artist by vote of science-fiction fans

1954   Leaves, on a full-time basis, the science-fiction/fantasy illustration field

1963   Paints last piece in the field—Cover for *The Magazine of Fantasy & Science-Fiction* "A Rose for Ecclesiastes"

1964   April 11th Hannes Bok dies of an apparent heart attack

Introduction
by Stephen D. Korshak

In the early 1920's, professional magazines specializing in science fiction and fantasy began to appear in the United States. By 1939, when Hannes Bok made his professional debut, the field was populated by pulp magazines — inexpensive publications printed on cheap, uncoated paper with garish color covers and sketchy line drawings inside. Because the quality of pulp paper was "only a slight step above bathroom tissue and blotting paper...it was too soft and coarse to take ink properly."[1]

Hannes Bok's solution to these shortcomings was to stylize his pictures to compensate for the lack of subtlety that occurred when black and white drawings were reproduced. Bok began to use line work to create tension in a piece of art. Even though no overt action existed in a particular scene, through the use of lush outline curves, a feeling that movement had or was about to occur was suggested. The figures in his art became free flowing with exaggerated detail.

Bok's only formal art education was two years of art instruction in high school. In Seattle he painted murals in public buildings for the WPA, where in 1938 he met artists such as Morris Graves and Mark Tobey. The culmination of his artistic training was a visit to his mentor Maxfield Parrish.[2] Like Parrish, Bok sought to achieve the effect of stained glass in his paintings.[3] Parrish's technique of glazing made its way into Bok's artwork in the 1932-1938 period. This involved the application of one oil color at a time, then a coat of varnish, then another oil color, another coat of varnish and so forth.

The apex of Bok's professional career was between 1939 and 1954. His production of artwork was quite modest. This was due to his constant dispute with editors and publishers over pay, deadlines and artistic control and the slow meticulous procedure involved in the glazing process. Other contributing factors were his erratic work habits, and his other interests as writer, lithographer, woodcarver, occult philosopher and voluminous correspondent.

Bok's efforts to branch out of the pulp field were unsuccessful, as evidenced by the 1945 showing of his best paintings at the Ferragil Gallery in Manhattan. By 1954 the pulp magazine era was dying and Bok's job market was drying up. Eventually, after years of frustration and neglect, Bok admitted defeat. The man once described by friends as elfin, whose earlier artwork had displayed so much whimsy became a bitter cynic. Bok turned increasingly to mysticism and occult philosophy. His artwork took on a mystical dimension as he began painting madonnas, mandalas and occultist works.

On April 11, 1964 at 49 years of age, Bok died of an apparent heart attack. A recluse, "he died alone at night, unnoticed",[4] except for his beautiful artwork. If not for the efforts of his friend, Clarence Peacock, Bok's artwork would probably have been carted away by the building's superintendent to the nearest dump. But his work lives on to delight new generations with his unique and engaging style. Today, Hannes Bok is rightfully seen as one of the true giants of science fiction and fantasy art.

NOTES

1.   Hannes Bok, "Why Artists Go But Grey," *The Big O,* Les and Es Cole & Lee Jacobs, eds., August, 1951, page 22.

2.   Based on a letter Parrish wrote to Bok's friend Franklin Dietz on May 8, 1984, some writers have speculated that Bok never visited Parrish. In the letter, Parrish stated that he never met Bok but did receive letters from him. However, this letter was written when Parrish was 94 years old and perhaps somewhat short of memory. These writers have not taken into account the two valuable Parrish sketches mentioned below or the personally inscribed books from Parrish to Bok which exist. Finally in an unpublished interview conducted by art historian Robert Weinberg with fantasy artist Edd Cartier in 1990, Cartier mentioned that Bok definitely visited Parrish at least once and recalled some details of that meeting as described to him by Bok.

3.   A number of Bok's works have been examined and treated by the Florida paper conservator Maury Barlow Pepin. In the process, information was gleaned about Bok's materials and their handling. Mr. Pepin's notes include the following information:

Bok did thumb-nail sketches in pencil and artist's crayon on newsprint stock. A few of these have survived in his spiral-bound portfolios. Like those of many artists who work strictly for publication, most of Bok's finished black-and-white drawings and color paintings were done on commercial illustration board. This is a very flat, tough material which can withstand the repeated handling involved in the printing production process. Illustration board generally consists of an 1/8-inch-thick base of grey or brown solid cardboard stock, with a thin layer of smooth or slightly-textured white artists' paper factory-mounted on it.

Bok painted and drew on boards with either Strathmore cold-pressed kid bristol paper, or the smoother hot-pressed plate bristol. These hard-surfaced papers take inks and water-based media very well, and allow for complete control of surface texture by the artist. The paintings examined by the conservator were later works done in mixed materials, combining dry pastel and opaque gouaches with the oil-based fixative media and varnishes. Bok used to make his glazes. Judging by their resistance to fading over fifty years time and more, the pigments Bok used were of very high quality.

Bok didn't trust the entire reproduction process to the publisher's staff. He sometimes worked by hand on transparent sheets of acetate, creating overlays to give the exact background effects he desired. An impressive example of one of Bok's "Kodachromes of the impossible" is an entire four-color printing separation hand-painted by the artist on clear acetate. The effect is like looking at a stained-glass window.

The physical condition of surviving illustrations is what one might expect in what was basically an industrial situation. The two-inch margin outside the painting itself is often covered with printer's marks and notes in crayon or grease pencil. Tapes and adhesives of different kinds were used to hold the work for photography. Although these are interesting as records of the process, many of the materials, especially the tapes, have caused staining and other preservation problems. The art paper of the illustration boards is very dense and has so far resisted acidic stain-through from the mounting cardboard underneath. Preservation of such original illustration-board works for posterity will eventually require removal of the acidic cardboard backings from the facing paper. M. Barlow Pepin, 783 S. Atmore Circle, Deltona, Florida 32725.

4. Emil Petaja, *A Memorial Portfolio: Hannes Bok* (Bokanalia Memorial Foundation, 1970), page 2.

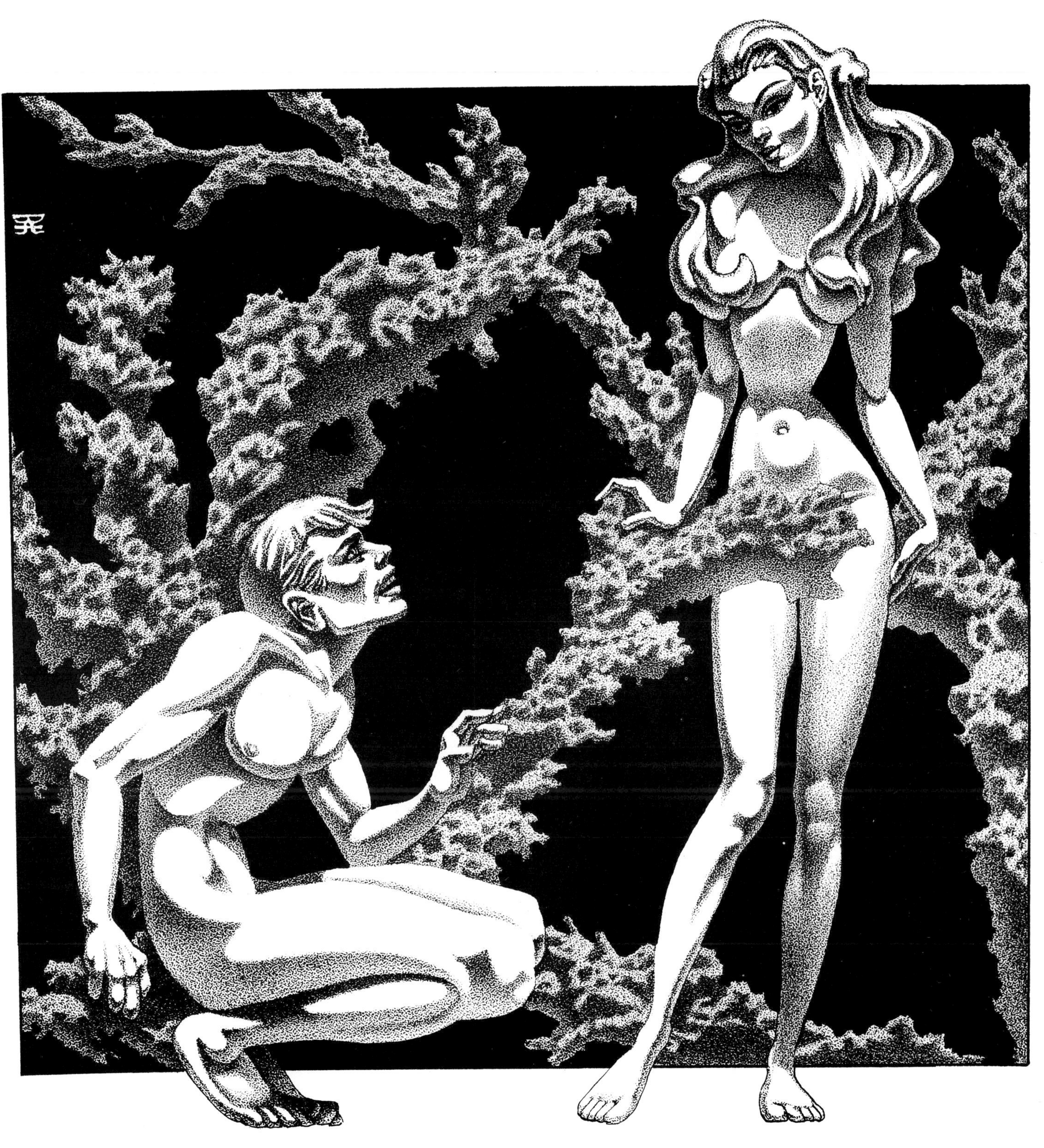

Illustration for "Red Coral" by Ray Palmer, 1951.

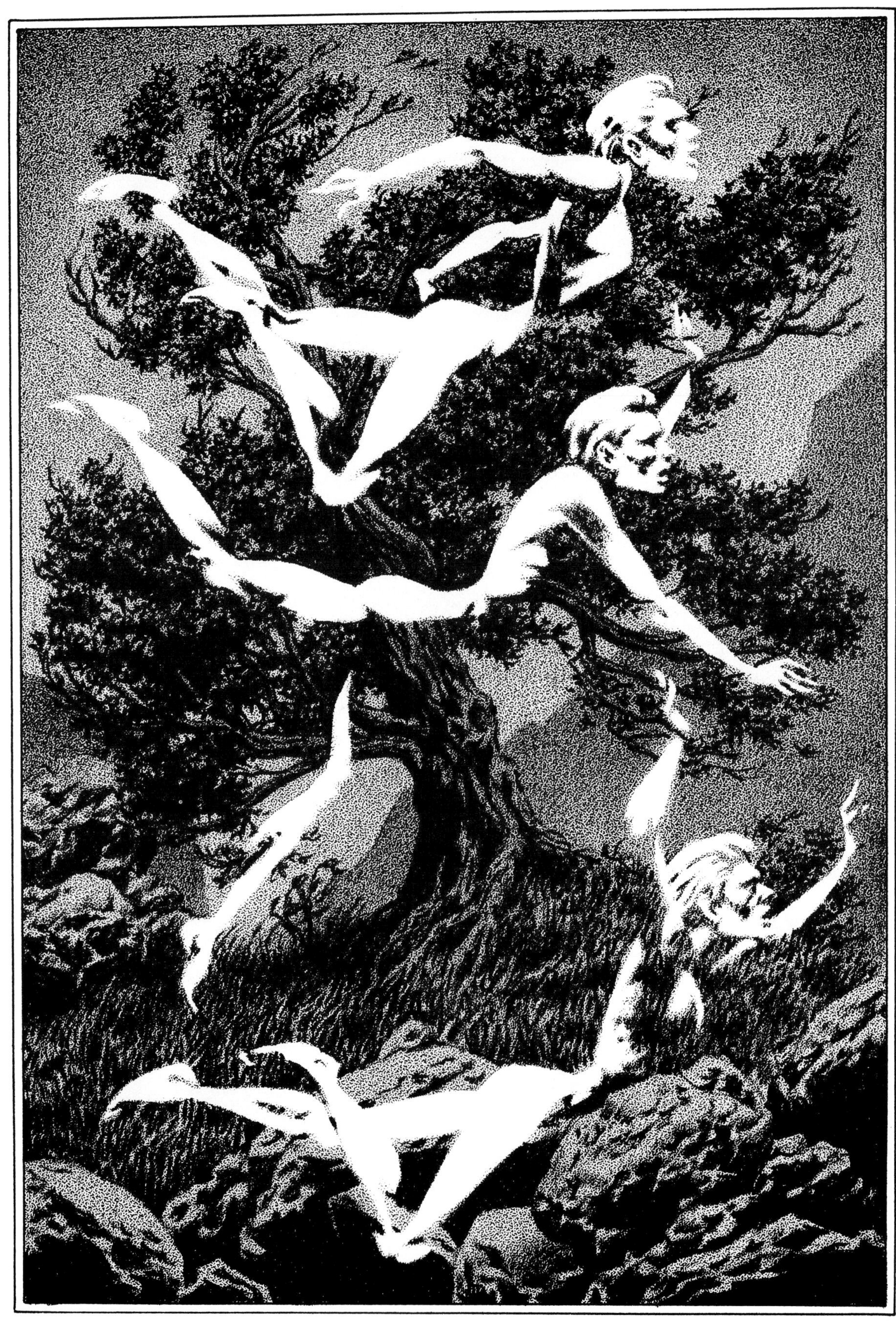

Illustration for "The Outsider" by H. P. Lovecraft, 1950.

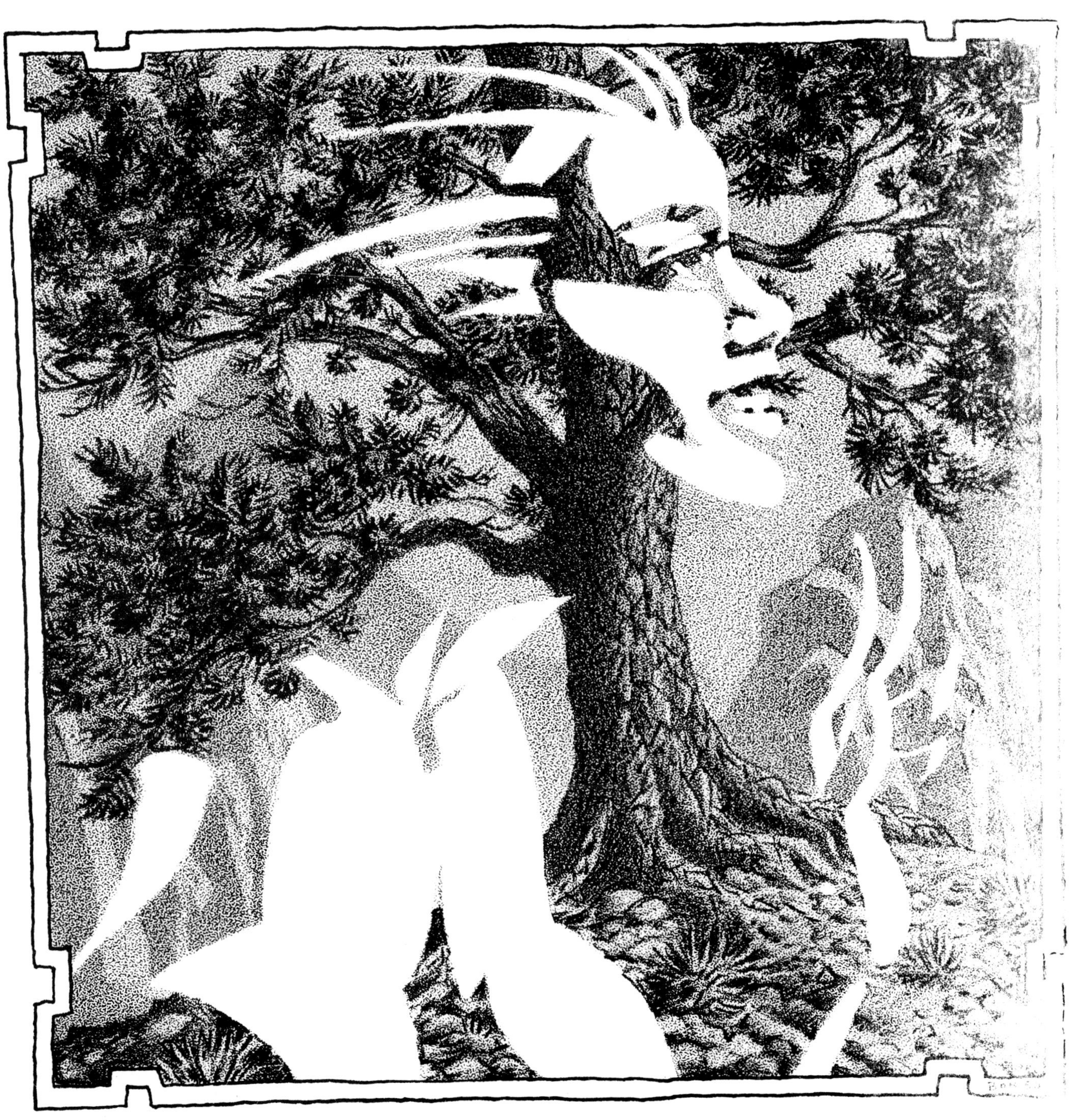

Illustration for "Image in the Pine," 1950.

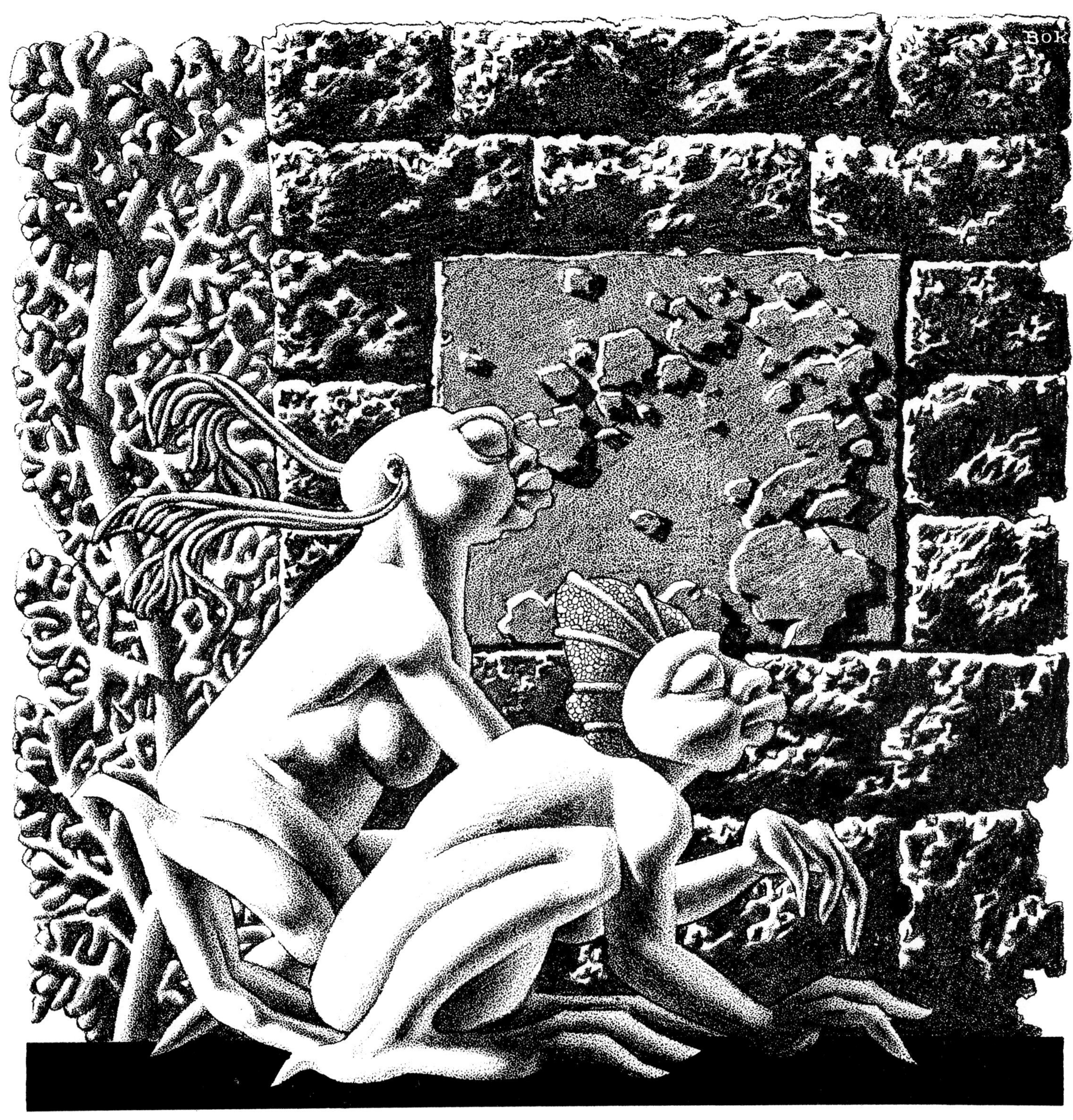

Illustration for "The Shadow over Innsmouth" by H. P. Lovecraft, 1942.

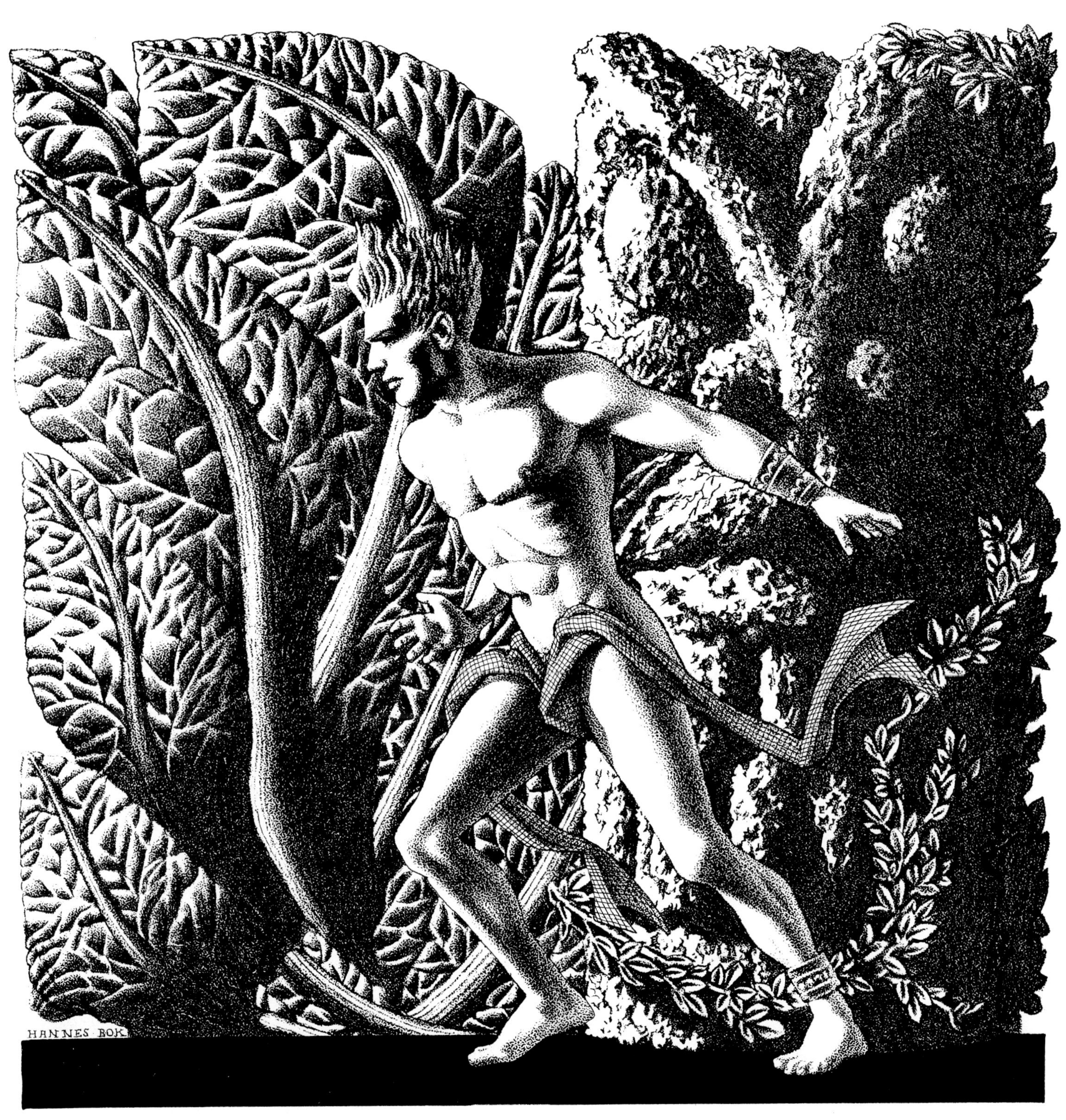

Illustration for "The Shadow over Innsmouth" by H. P. Lovecraft, 1942.

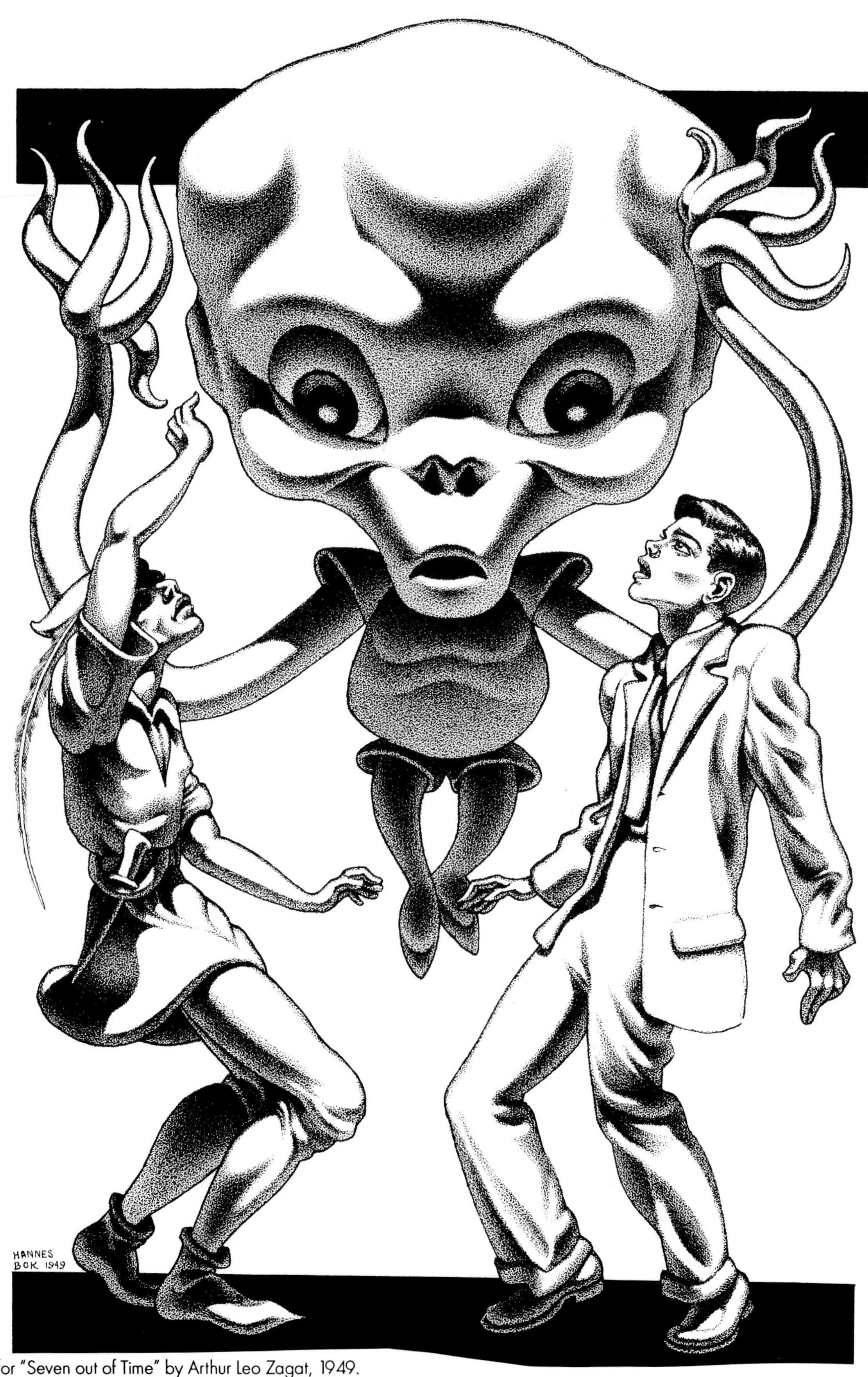

Illustration for "Seven out of Time" by Arthur Leo Zagat, 1949.

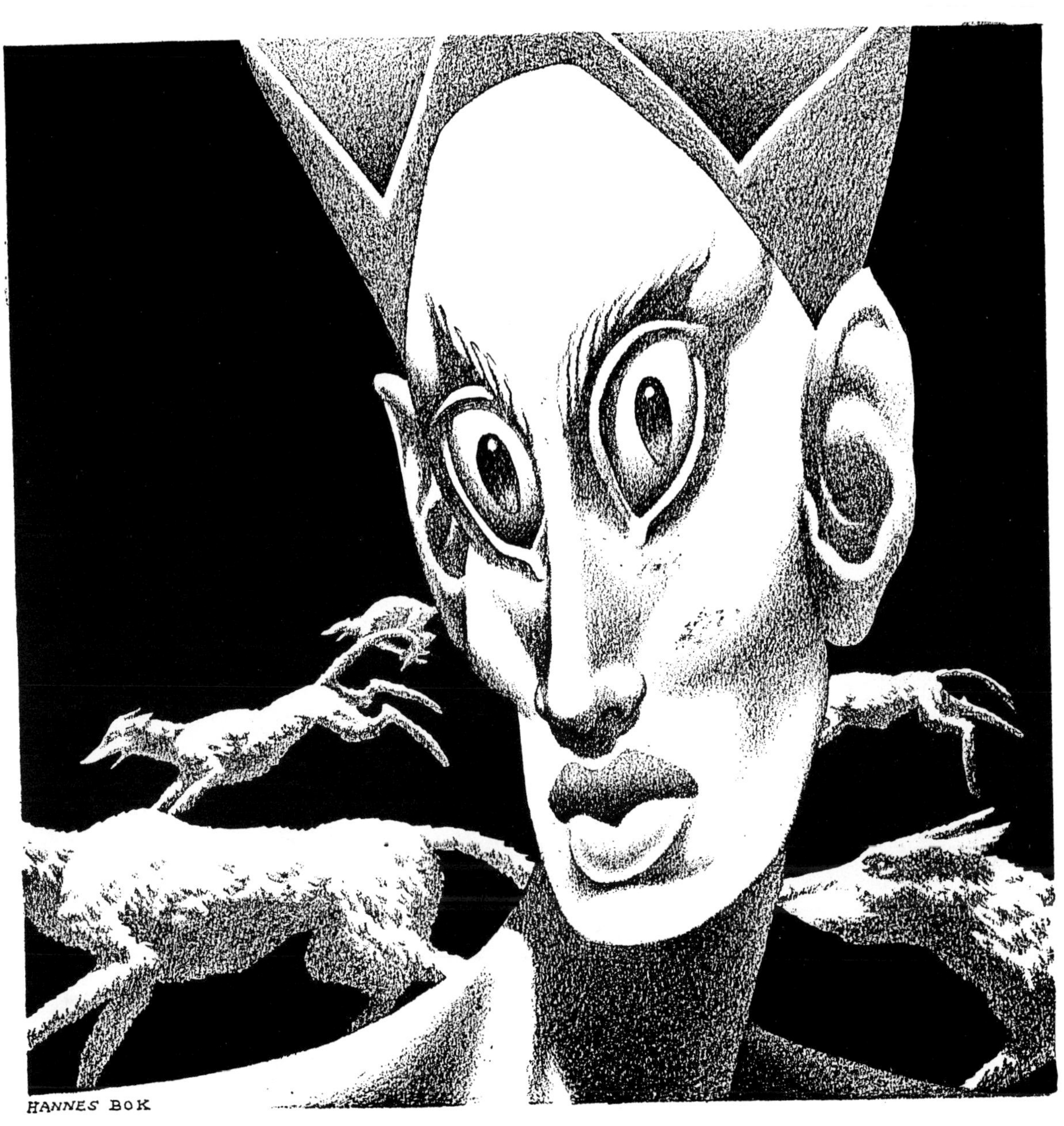

Black and white illustration

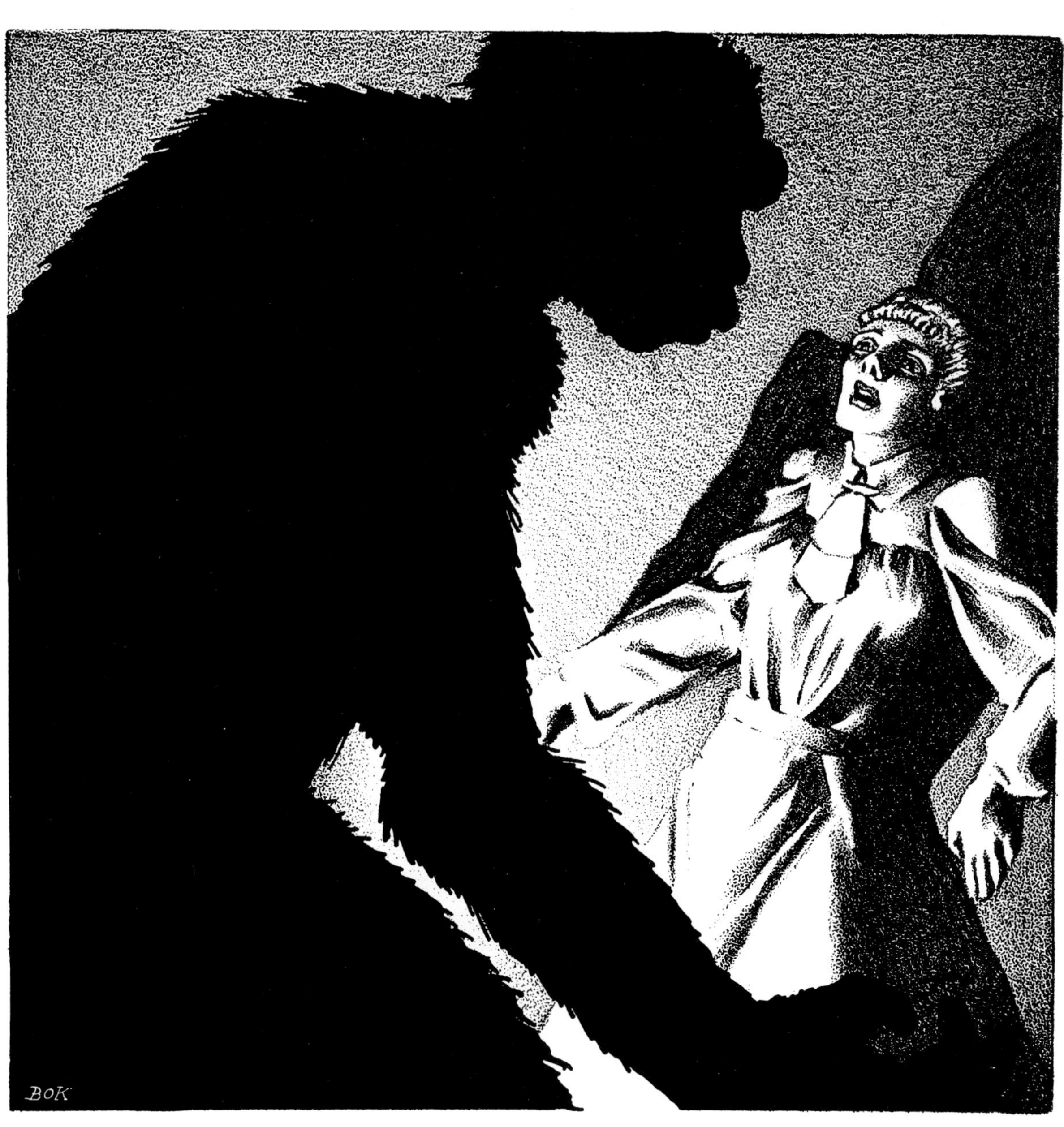

Black and white illustration

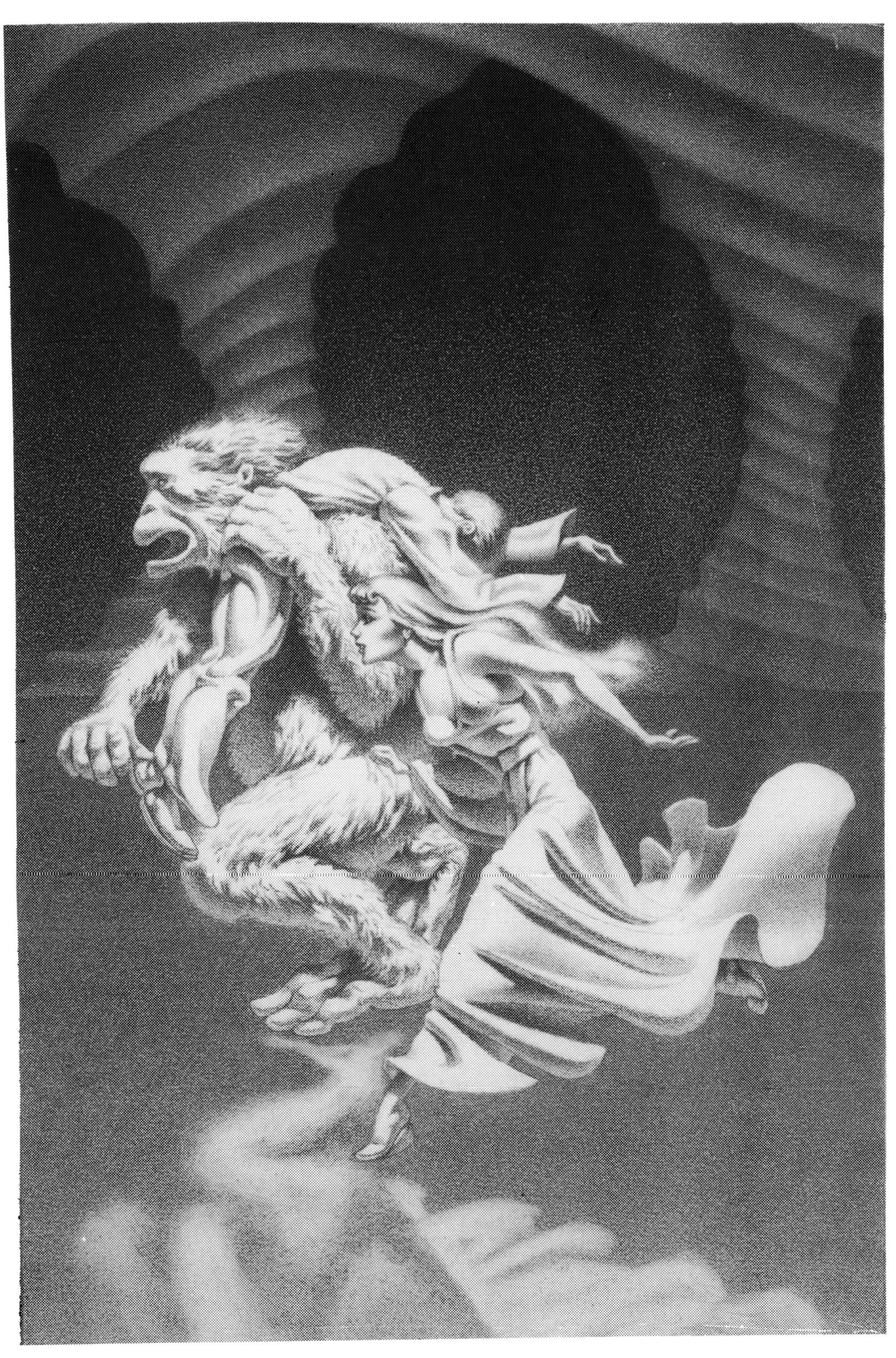

Black and white illustration

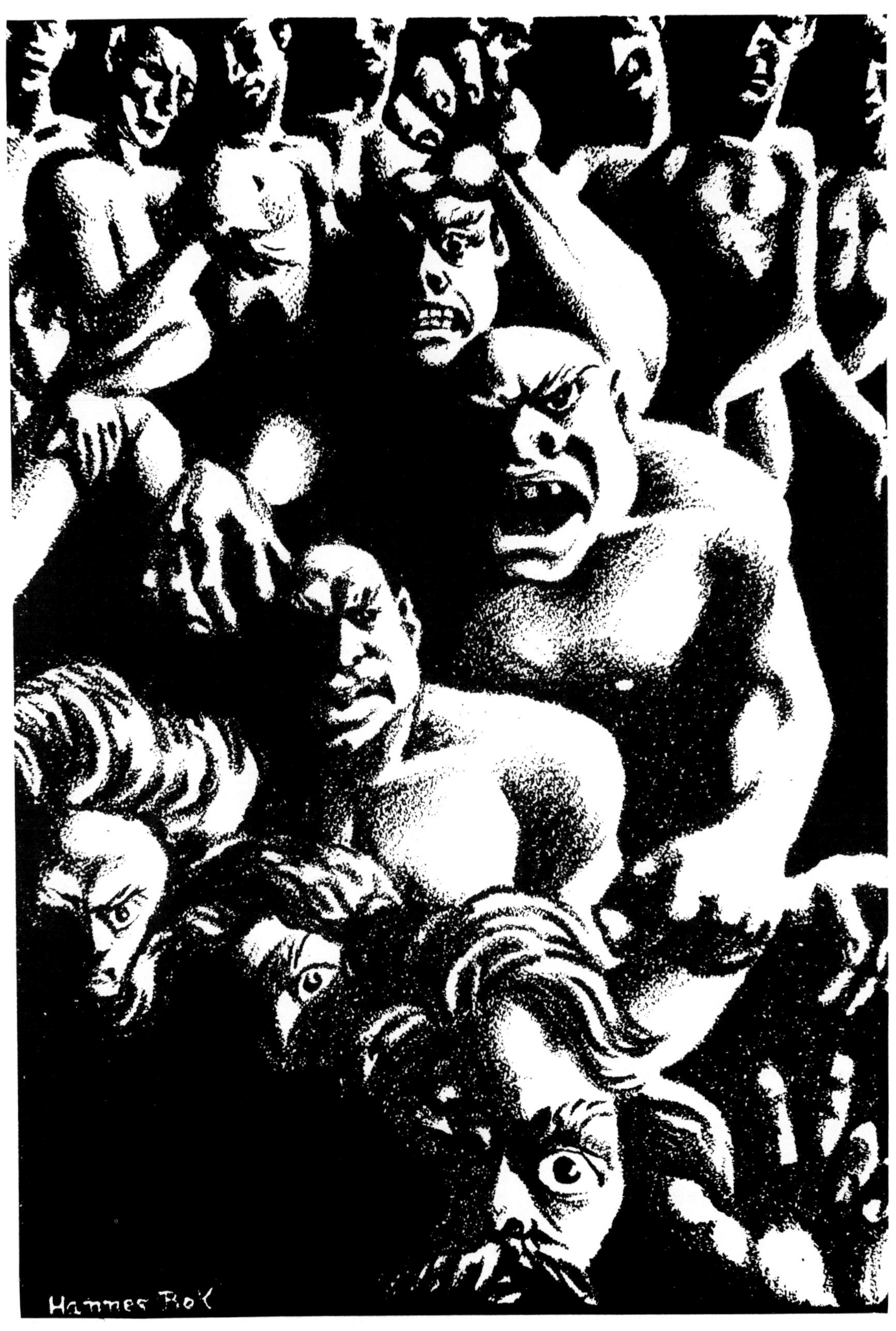

Black and white illustration

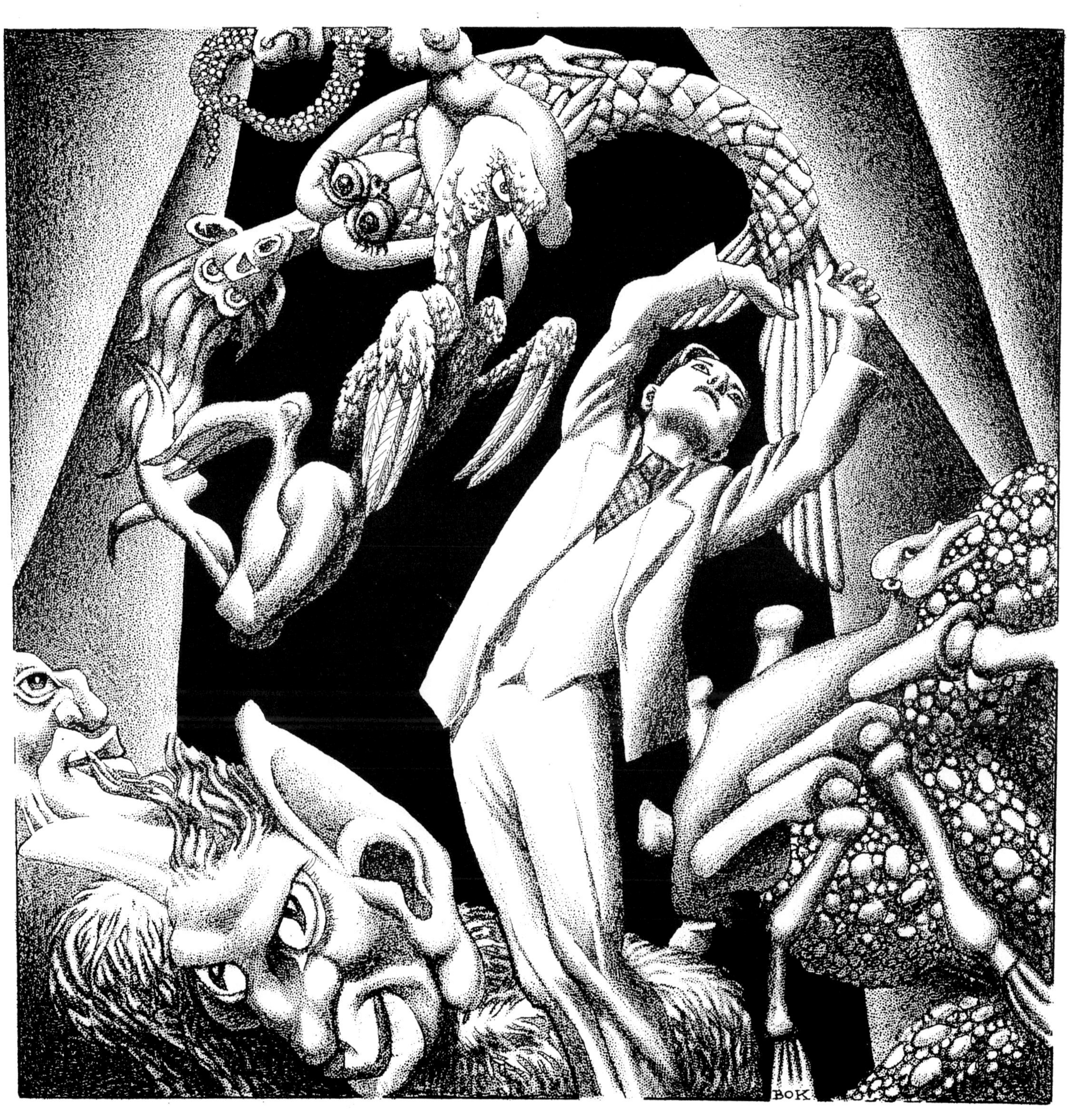

Illustration for "The Devotee of Evil" by Clark Ashton Smith, 1941.

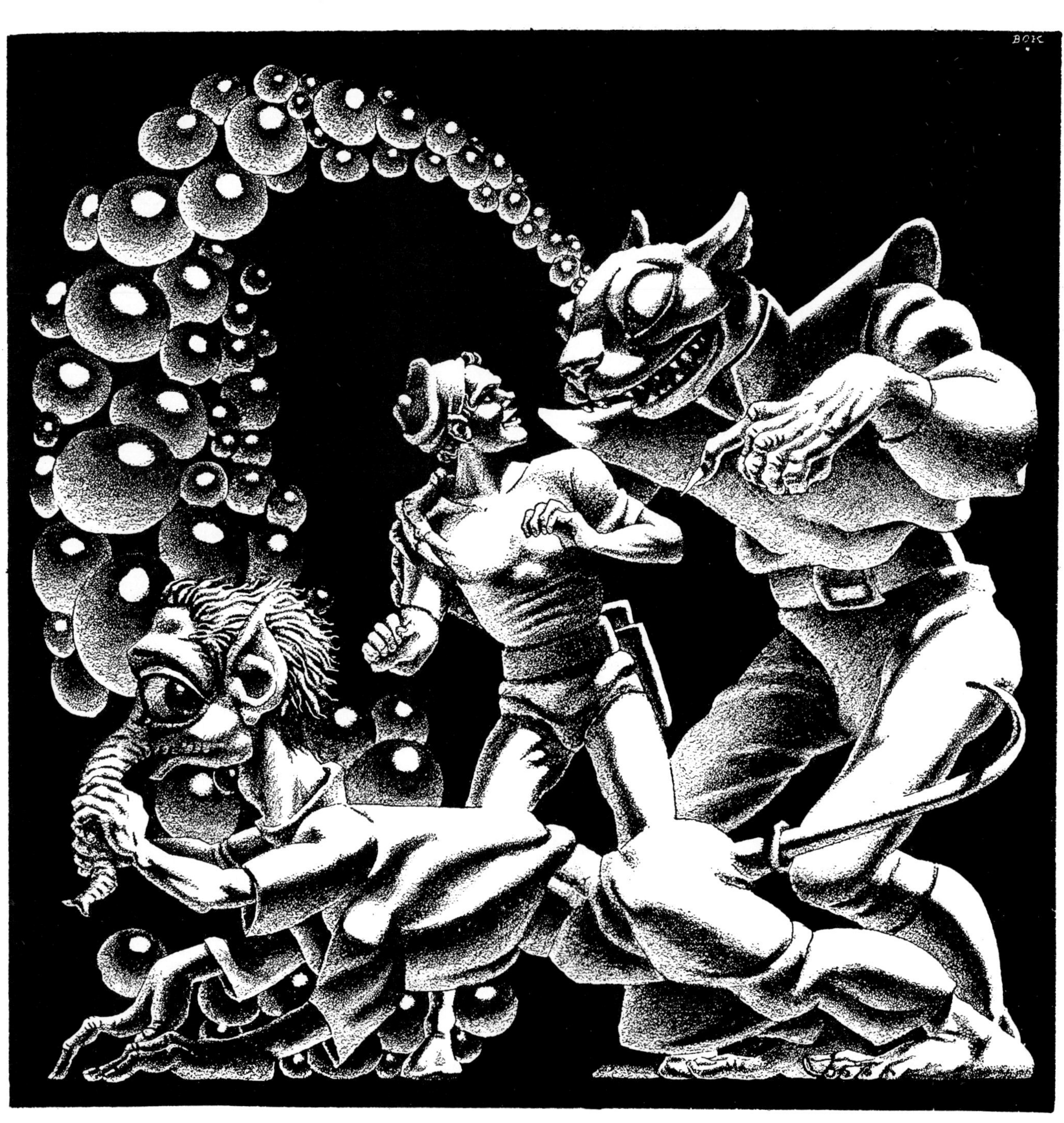

Illustration for "Planet Leave" by Clifton B. Kruse, 1941.

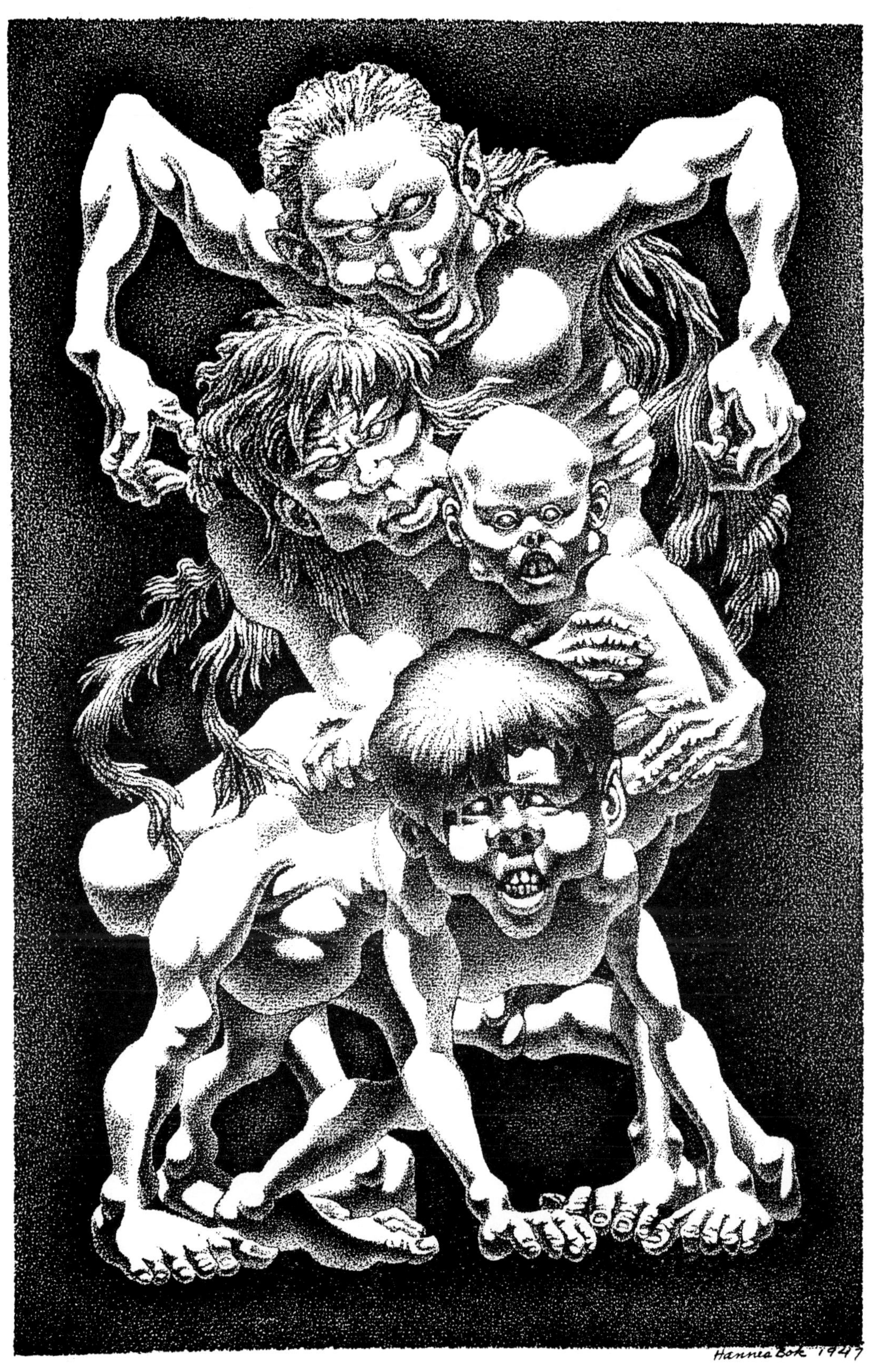

Illustration for "The Black Wheel" by A. Merritt & Hannes Bok, 1947.

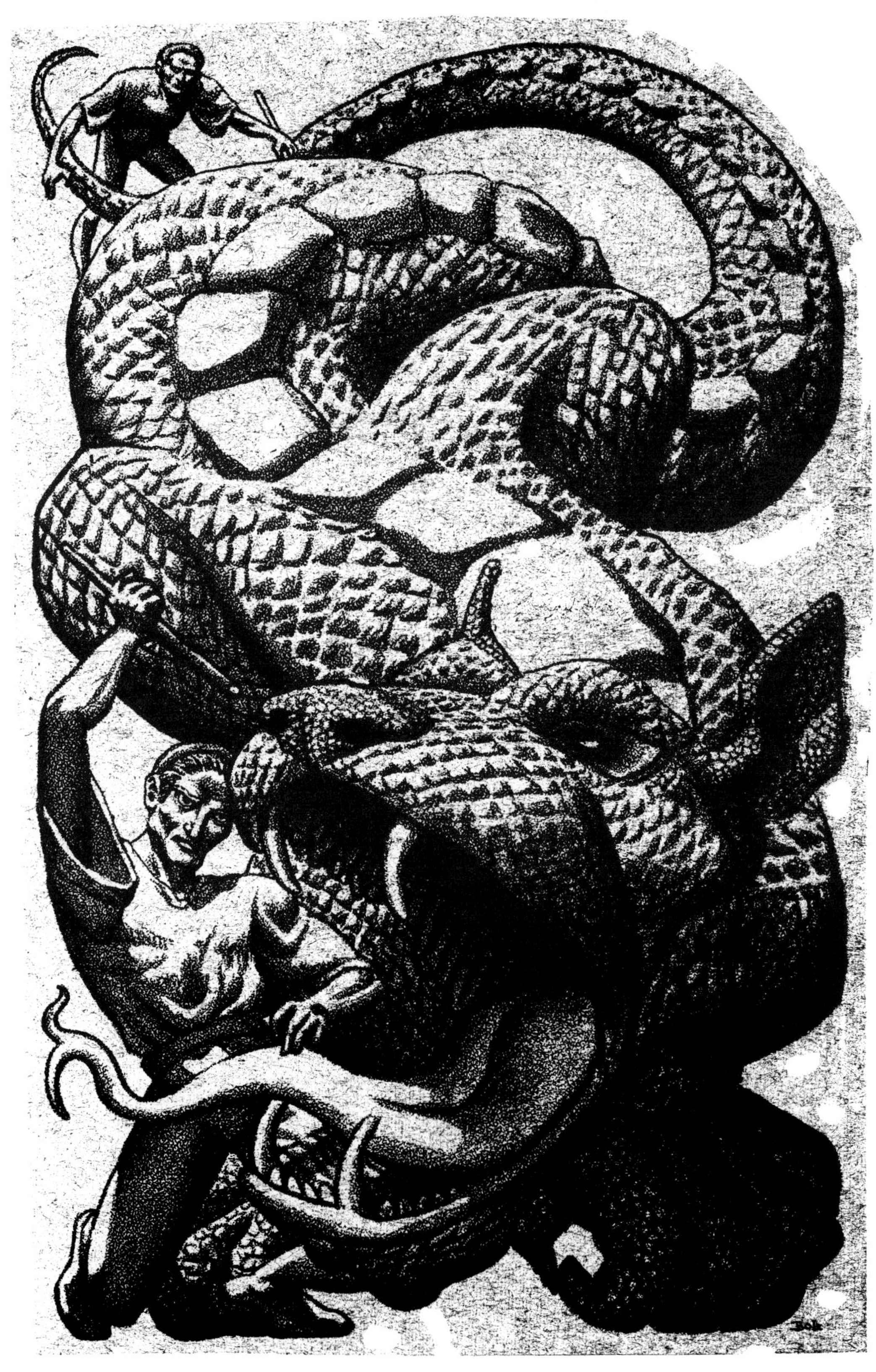

Illustration for "It's a Young World" by James MacCreigh (F. Pohl), 1941.

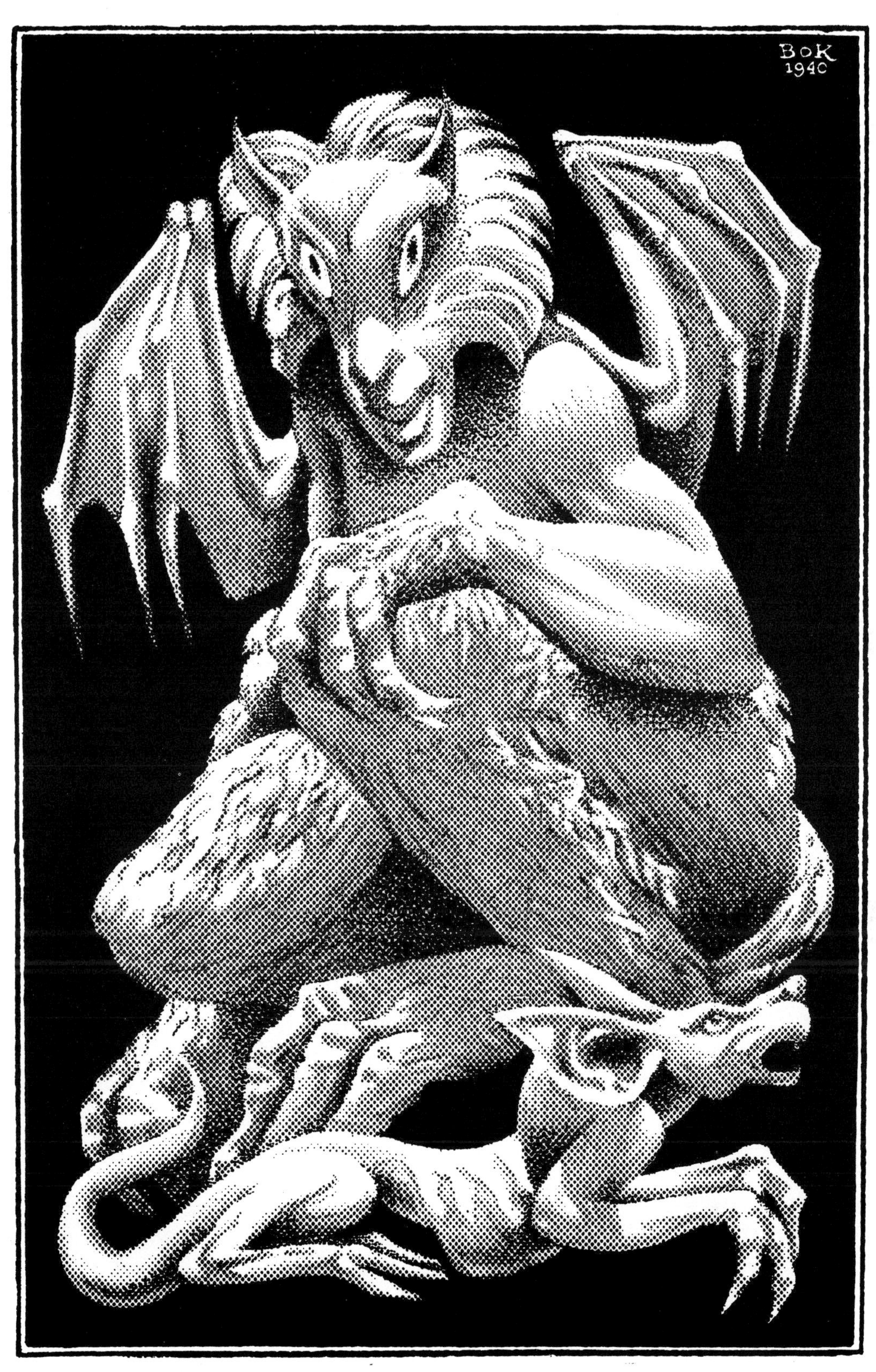

Illustration for "Something from Out There" by August W. Derleth, 1951.

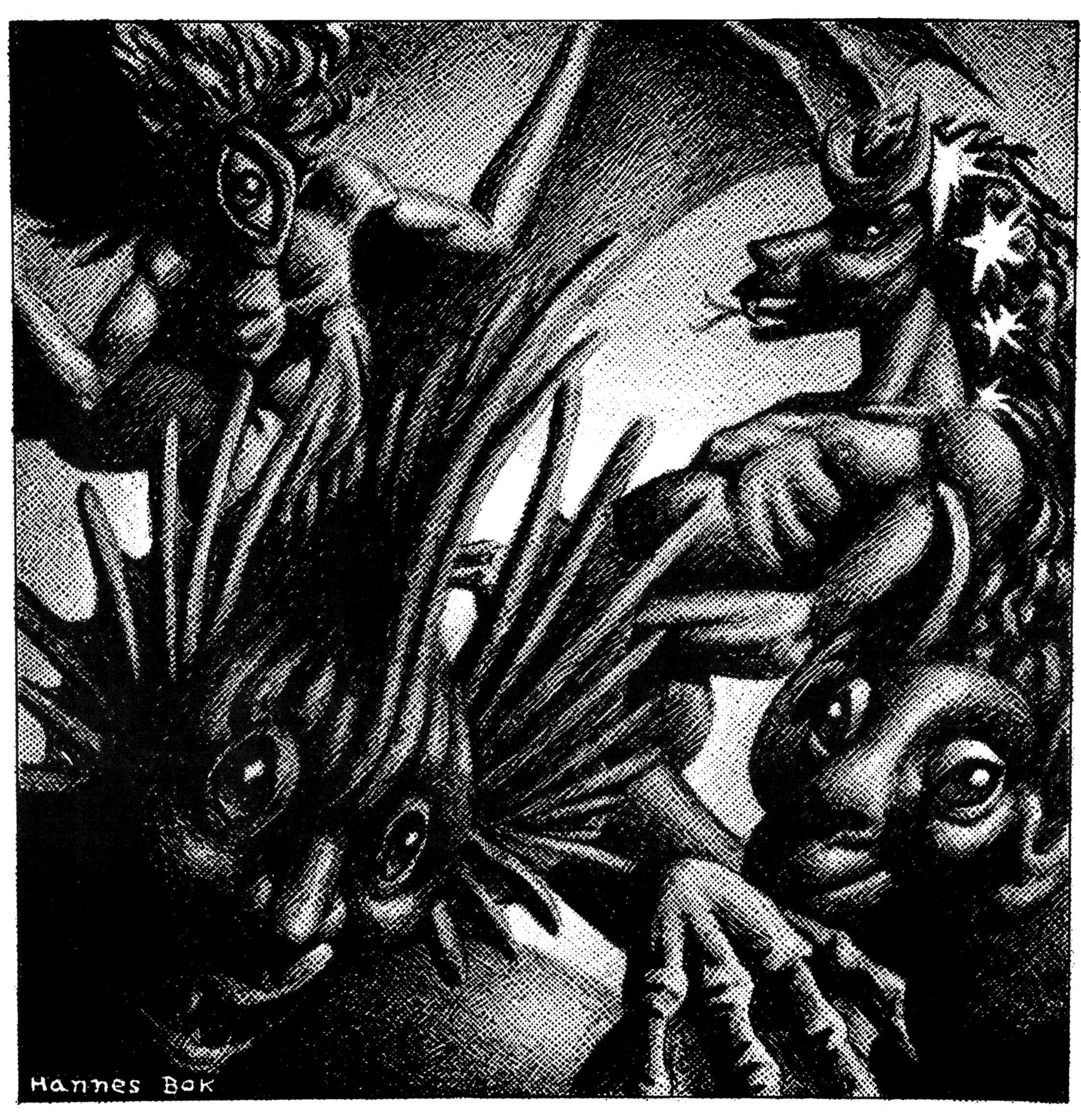

Illustration for "Horror in the Glen" by Clyde Irvine, 1940.

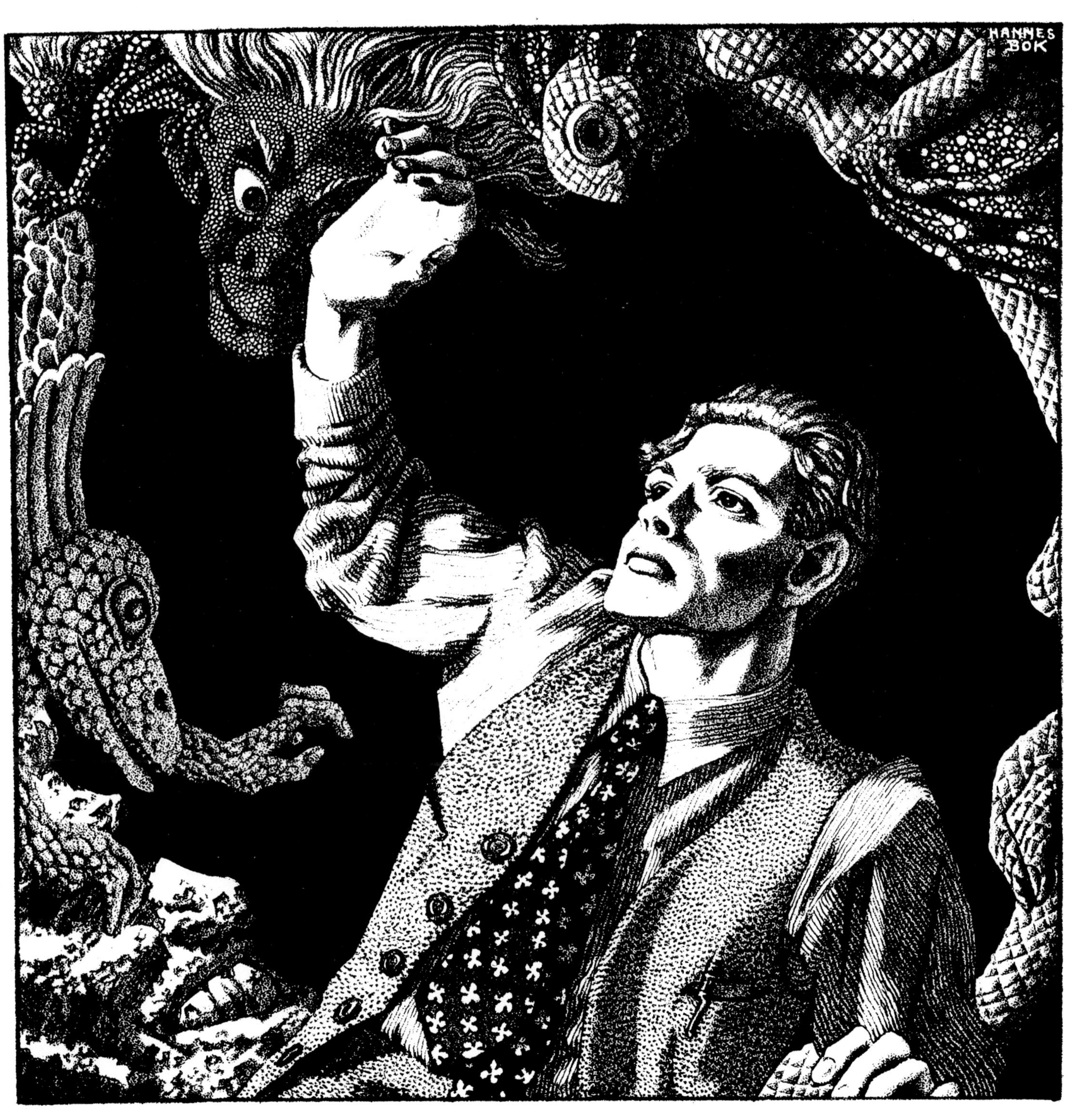

Illustration for "Master of Emotion" by Willard E. Hawkins, 1941.

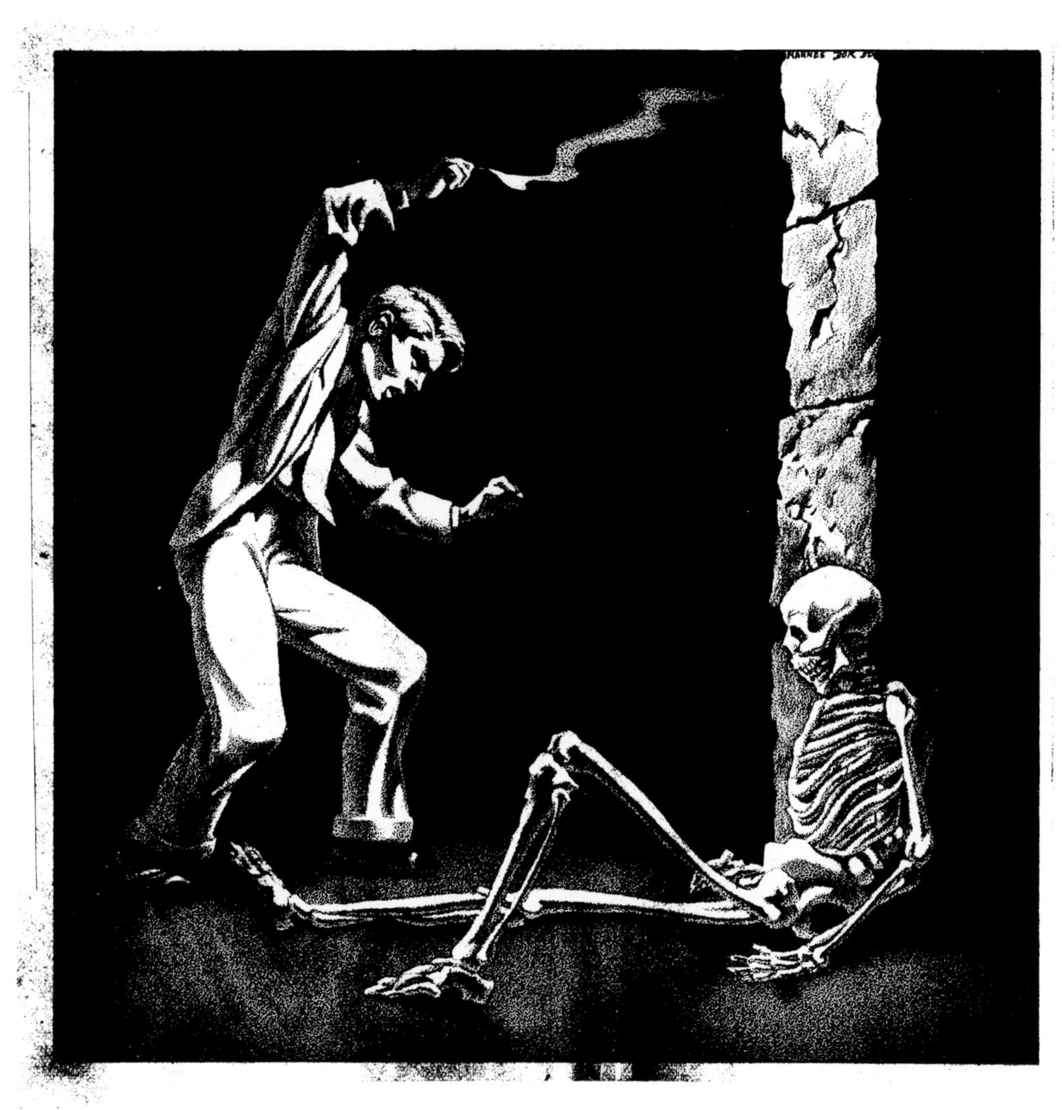

Illustration for "Cross of Mercrux" by Harry Walton, 1950.

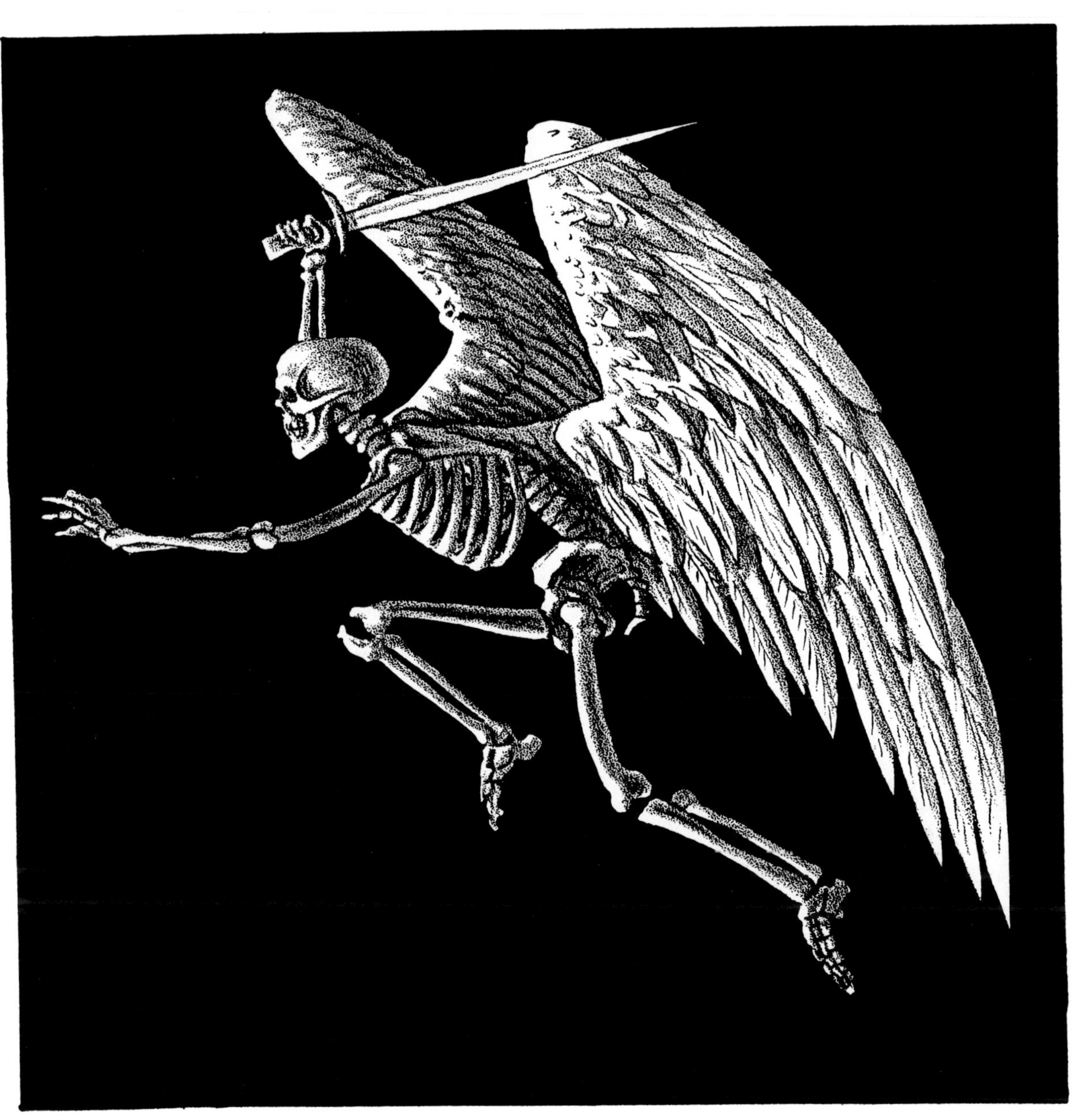

Illustration for "A Haunting Sea Tale" by Malcolm Jameson.

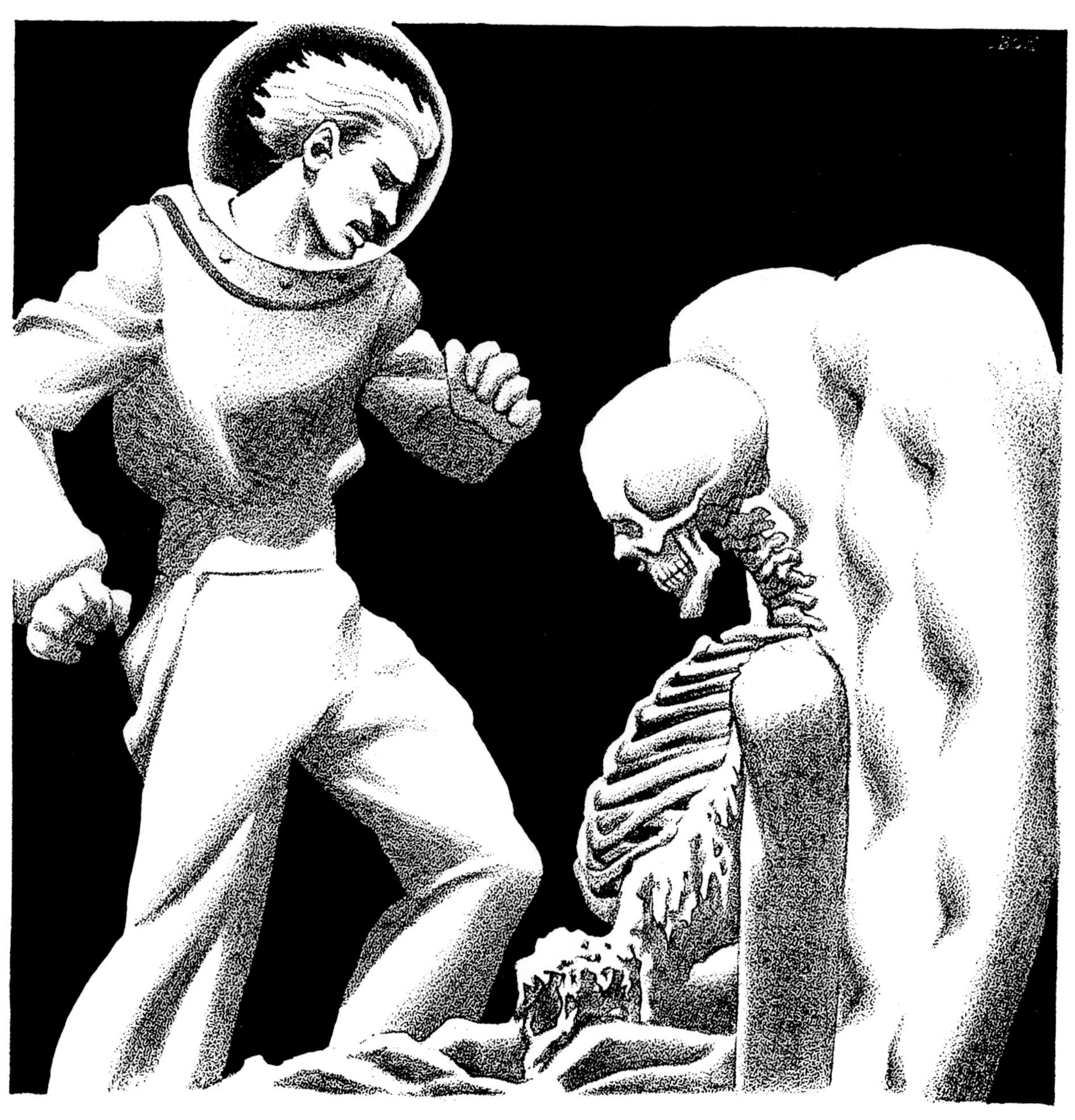

Black and white illustration

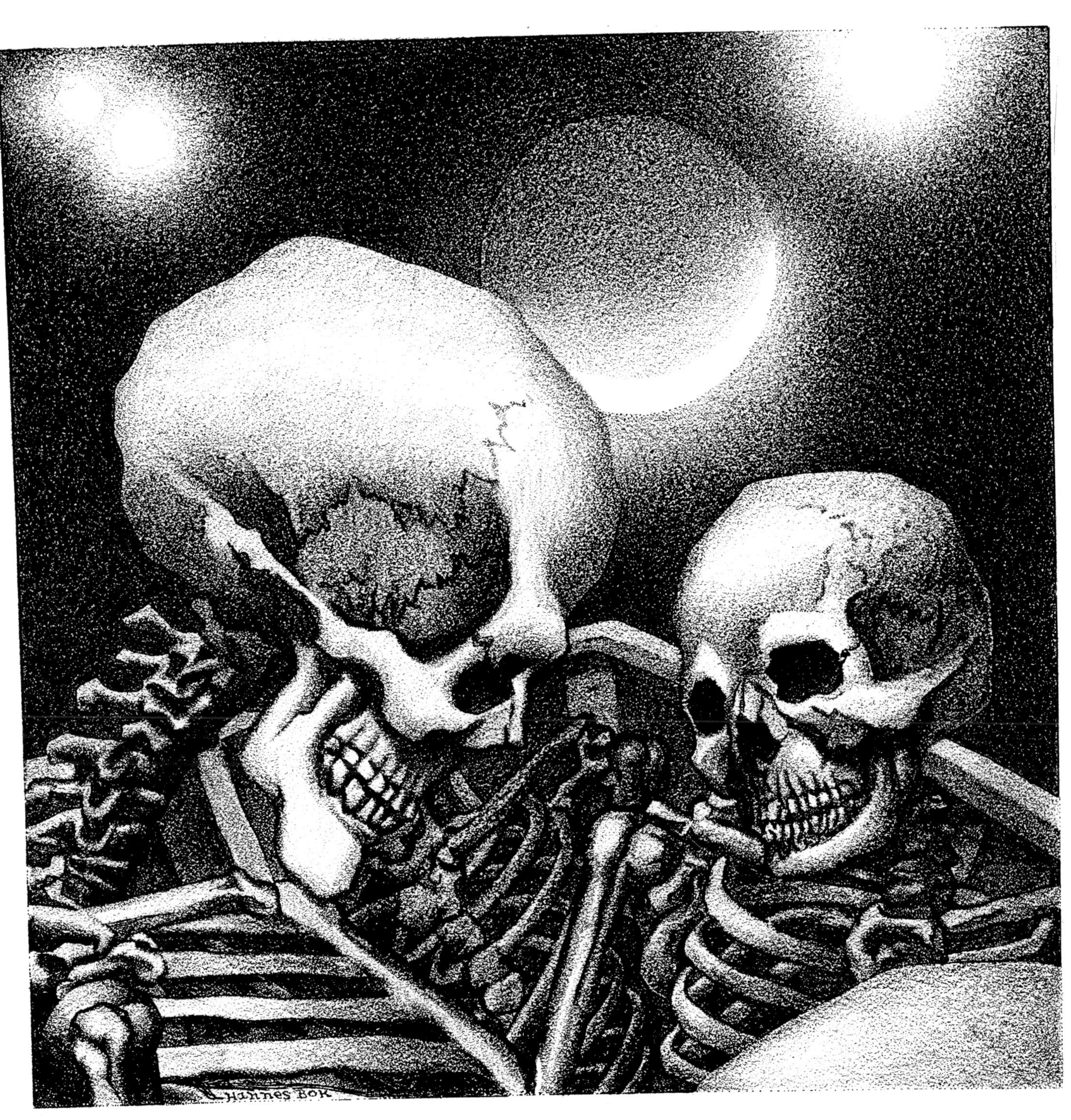

Illustration for "The Ship that Died" by John De Witt Gilbert, 1941.

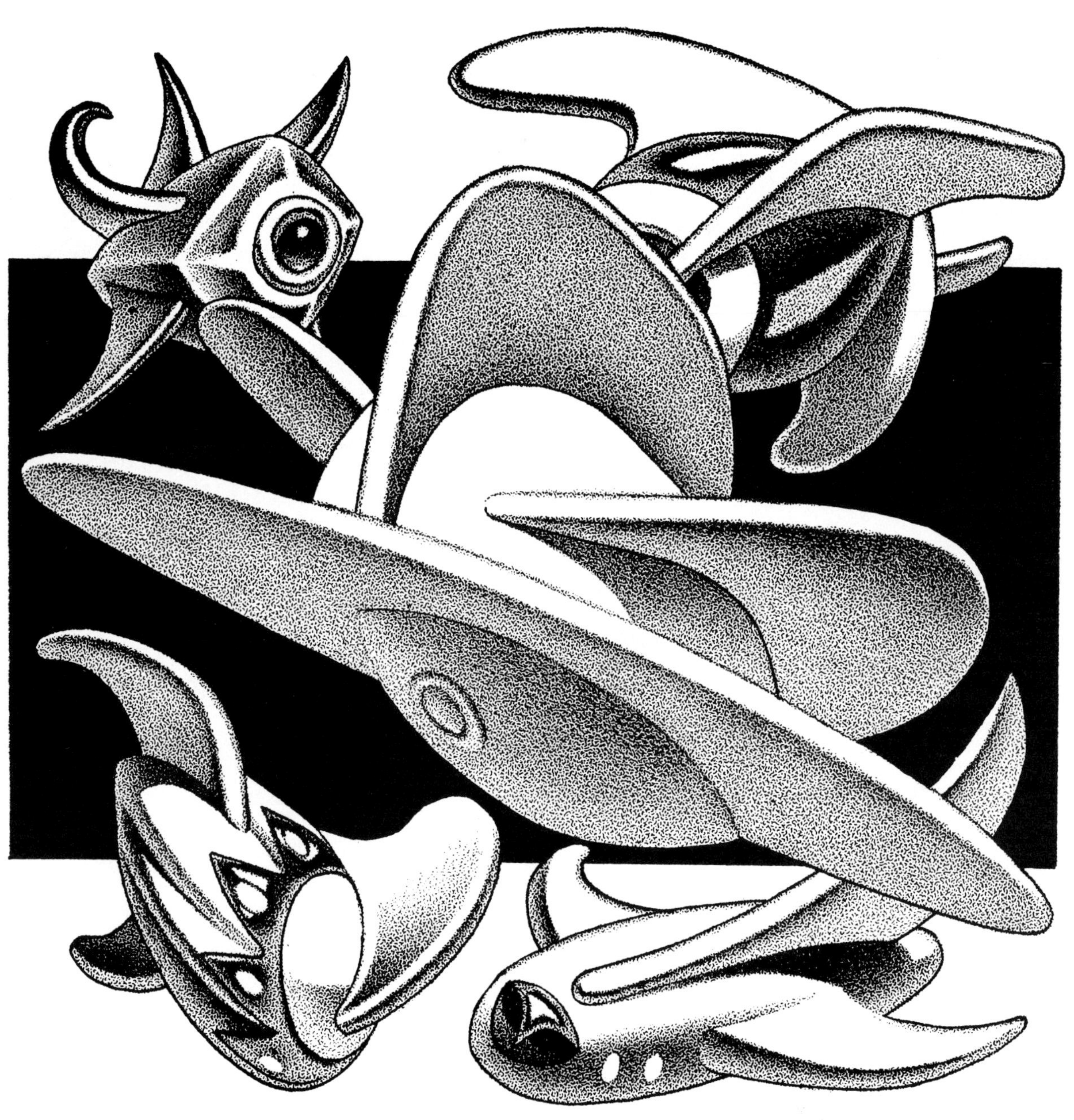

Black and white illustration

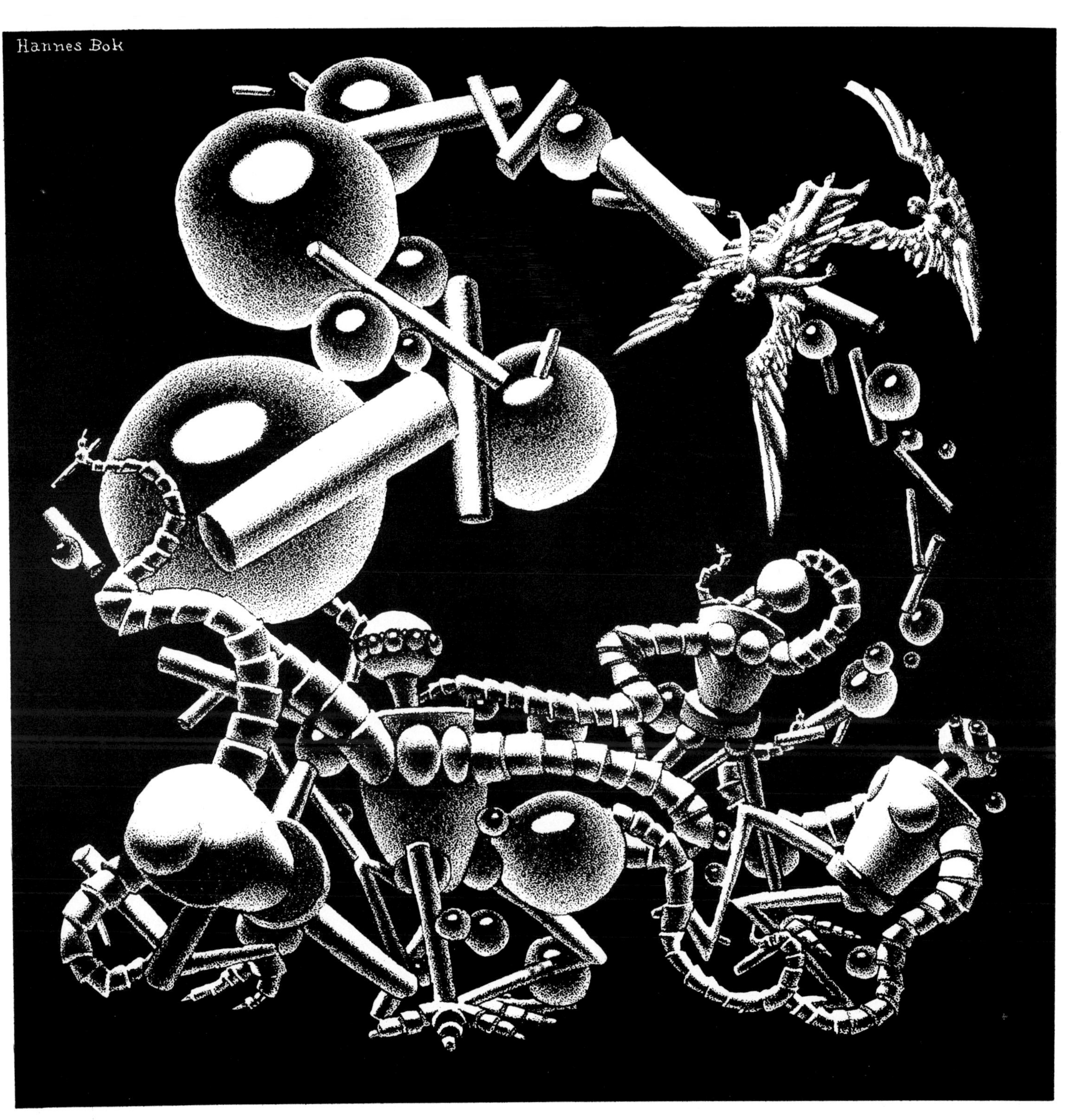

Illustration for "Space Junk," 1940s.

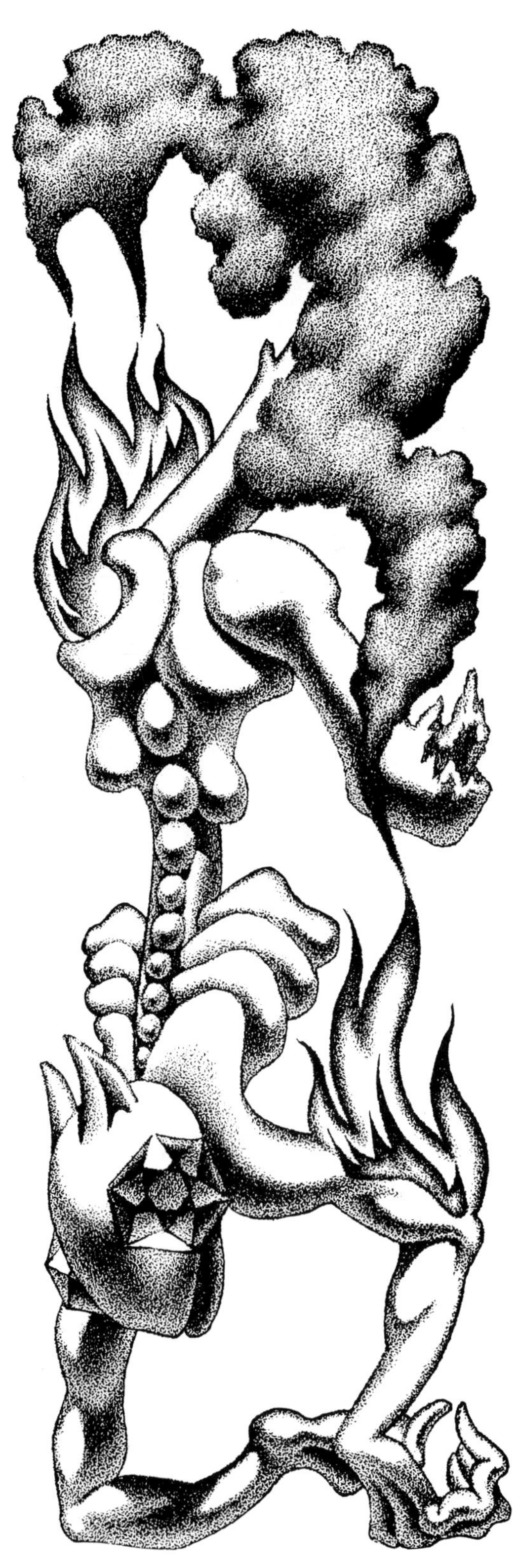

Black and white illustration

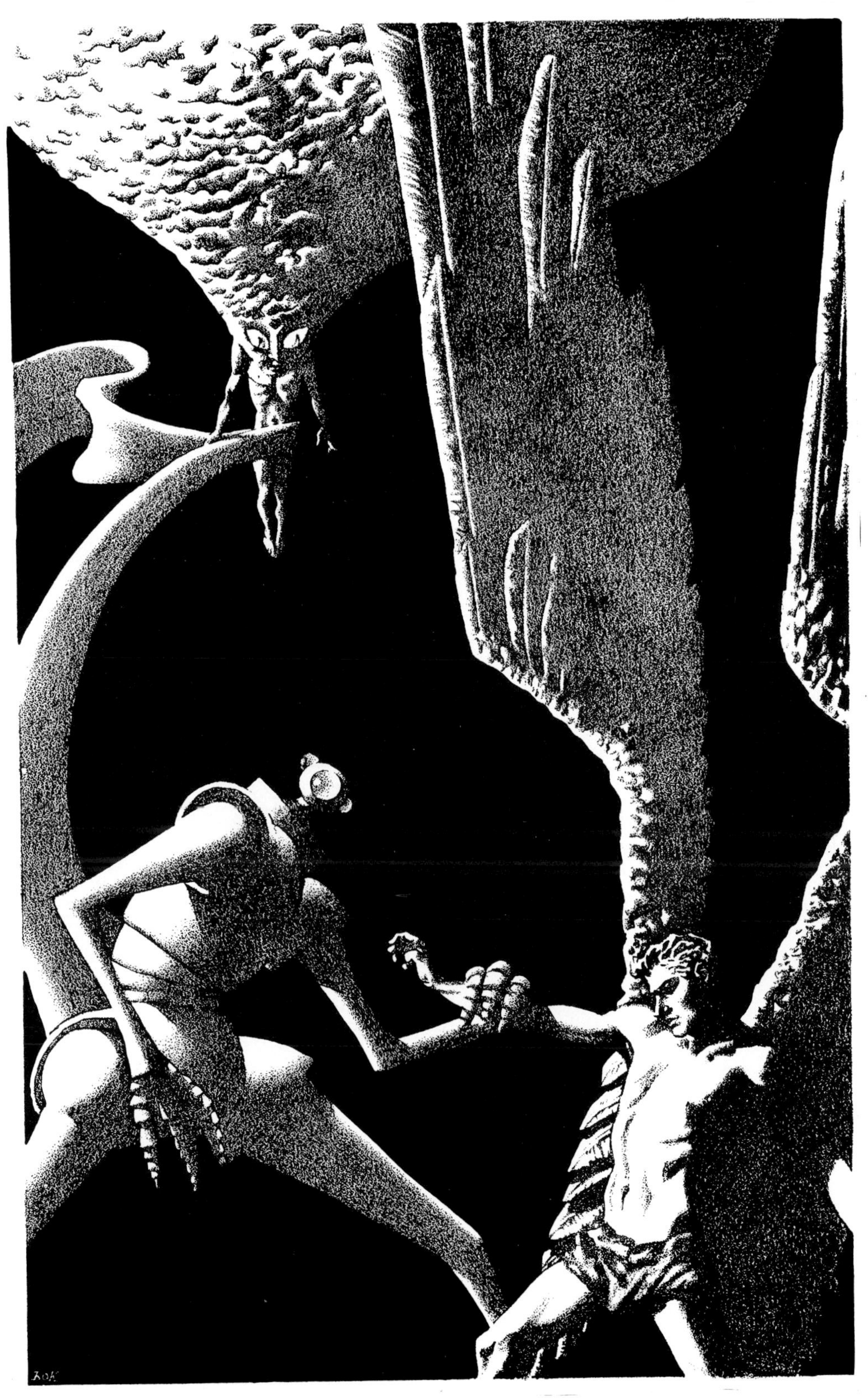

Illustration for "Wings Across Time" by Frank Edward Arnold, 1942.

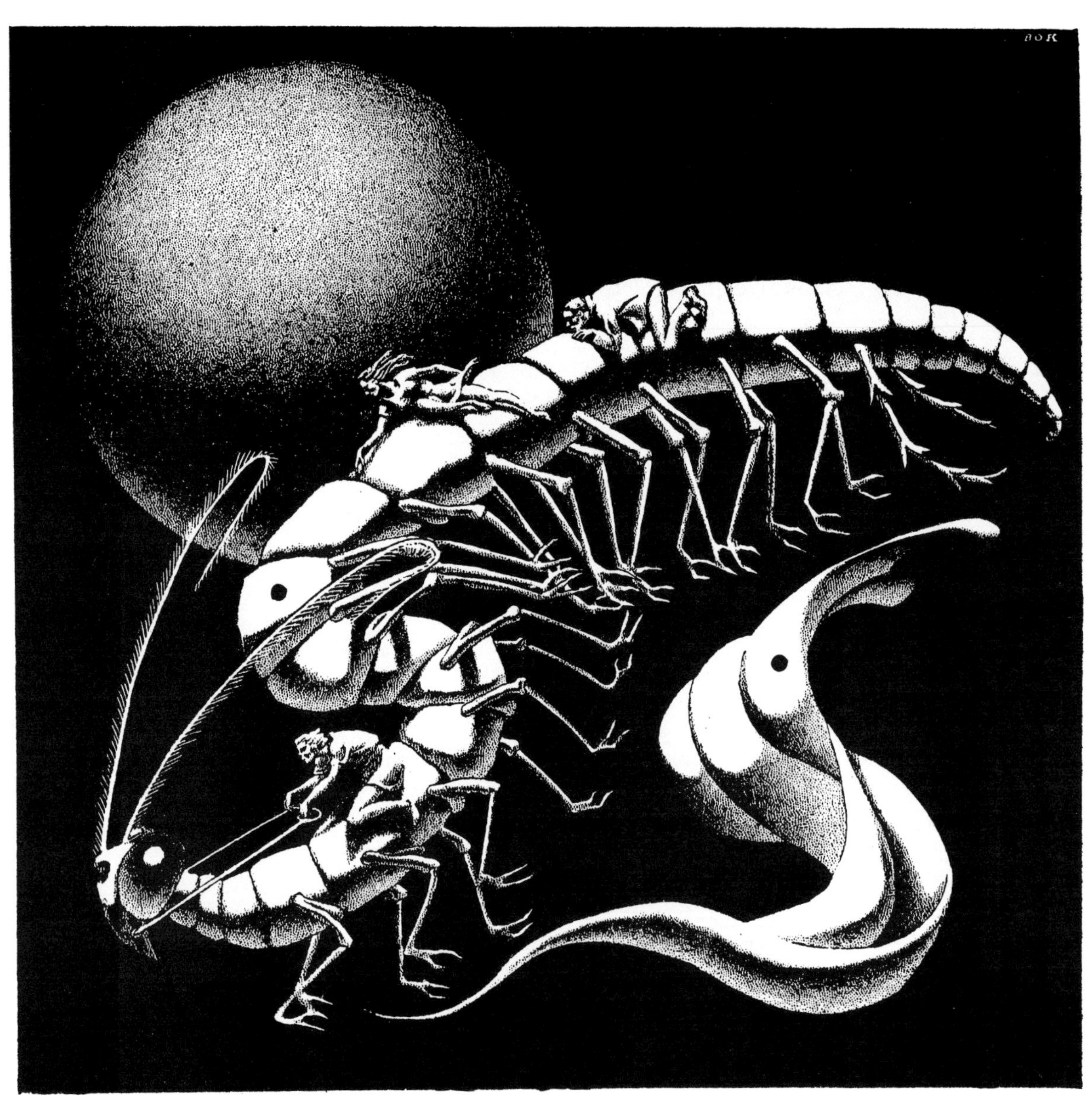

Black and white illustration

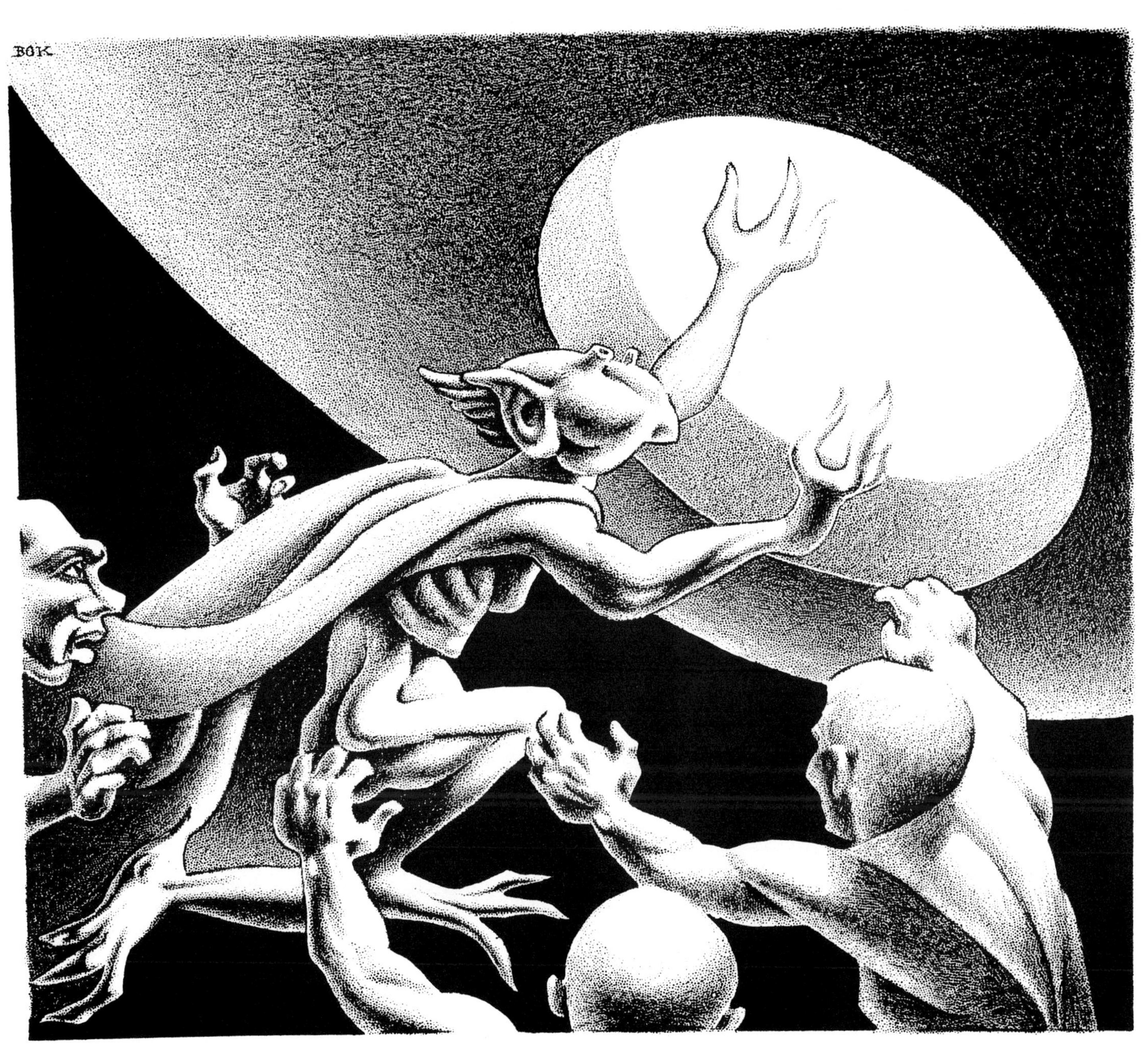

Illustration for "Another's Eyes" by John L. Chapman, 1941.

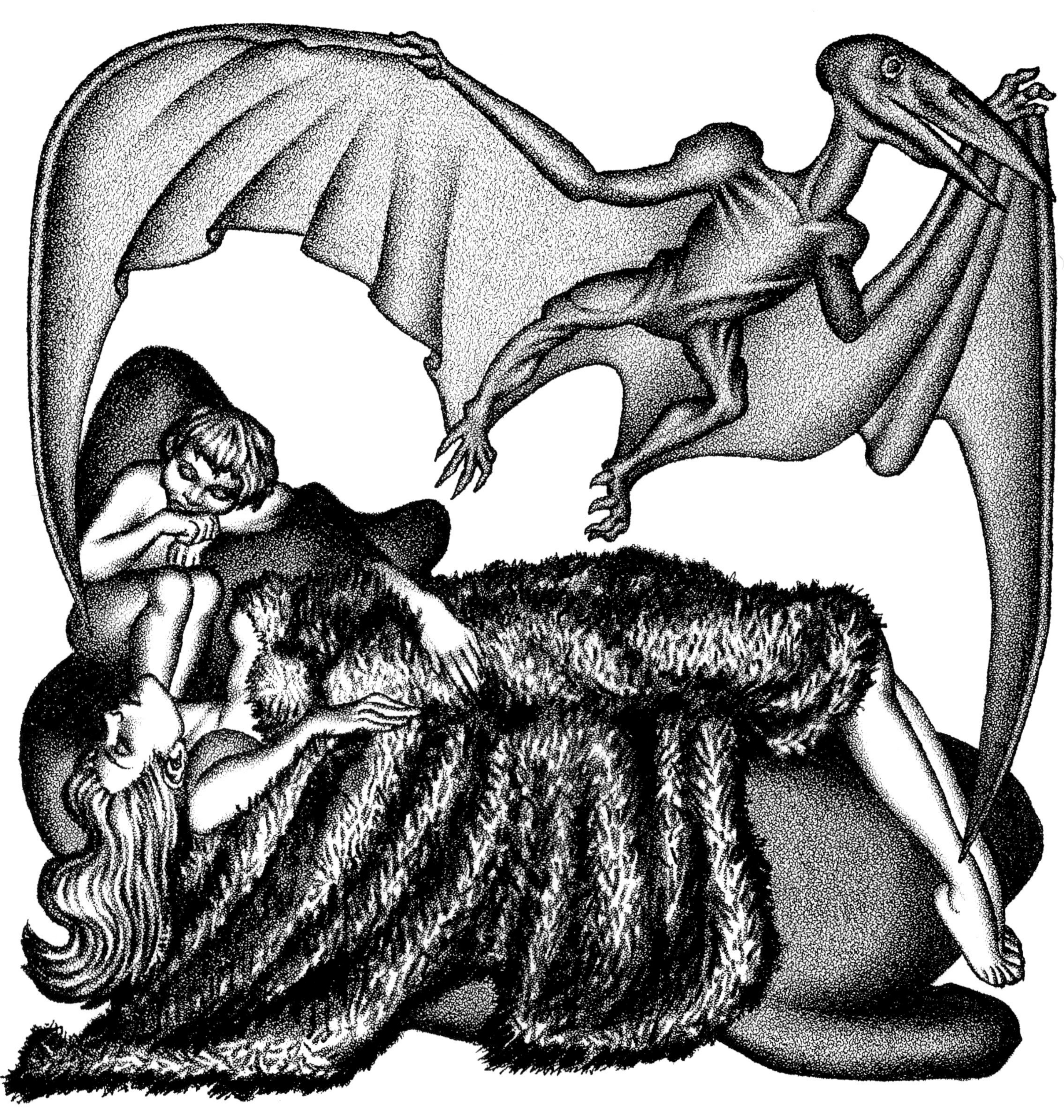

Illustration for "The Long Dawn" by Noel Loomis, 1950.

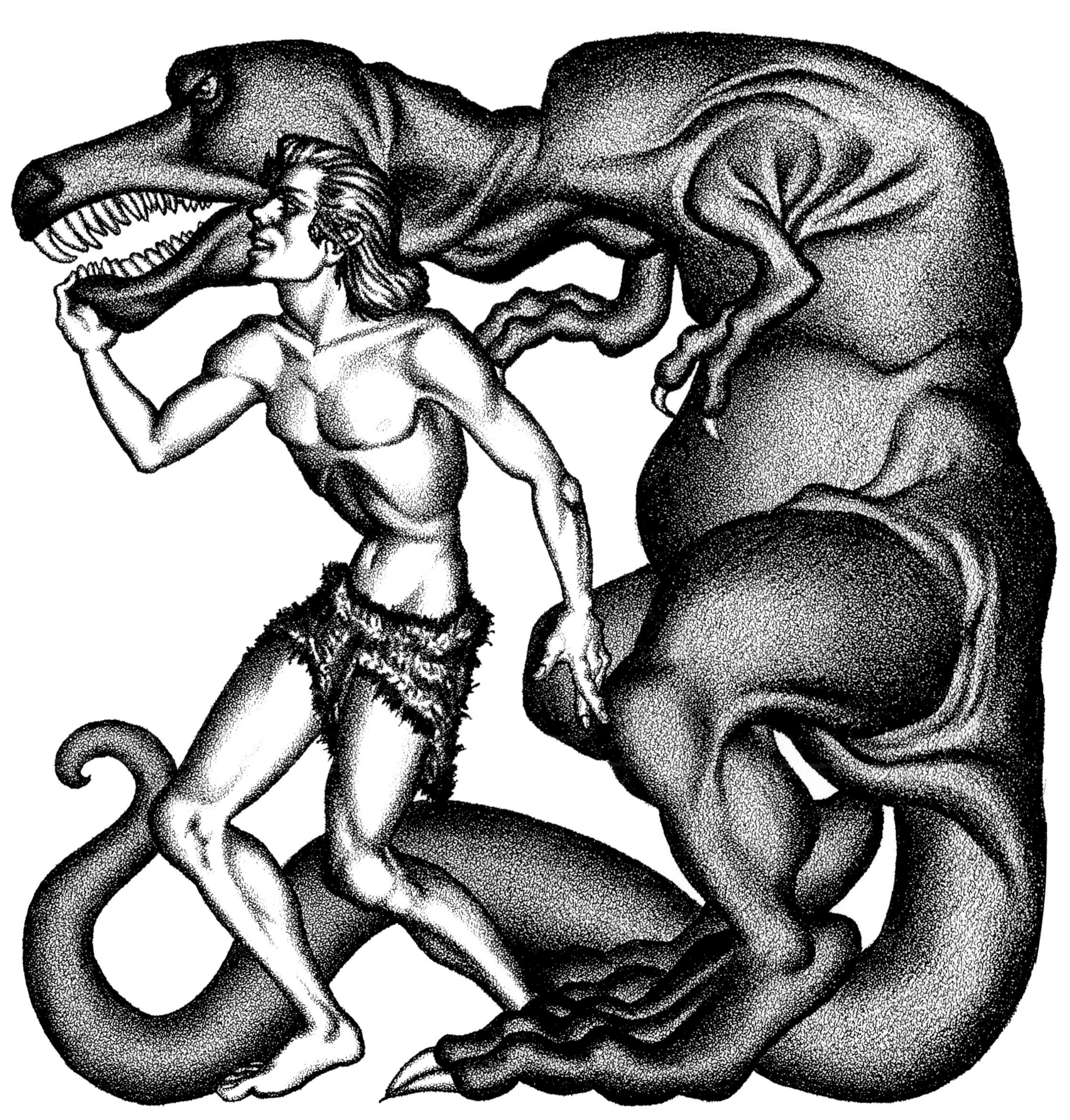

Illustration for "The Long Dawn" by Noel Loomis, 1950.

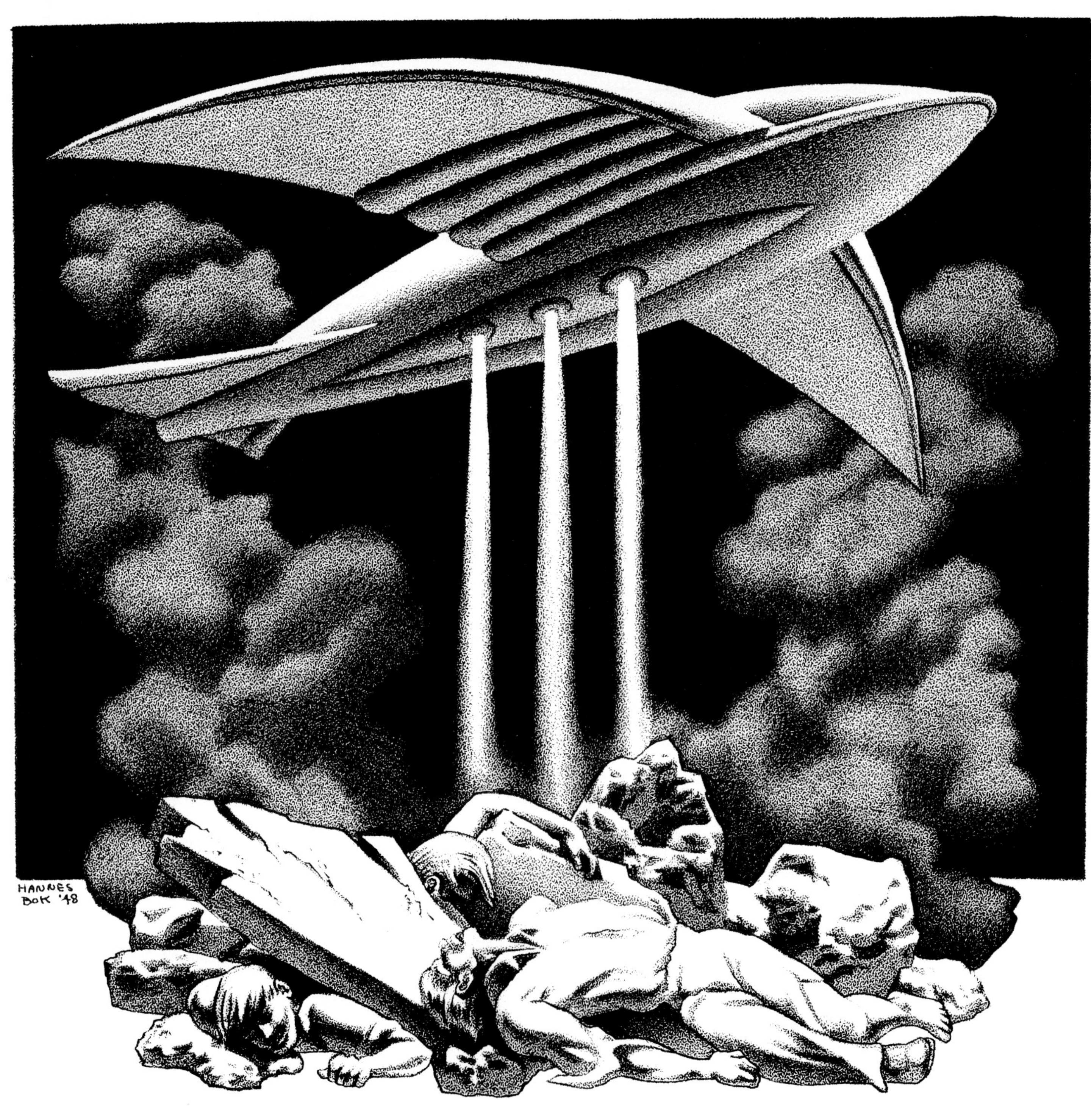

Illustration for "The Earth Killers" by A. E. Van Vogt, 1949.

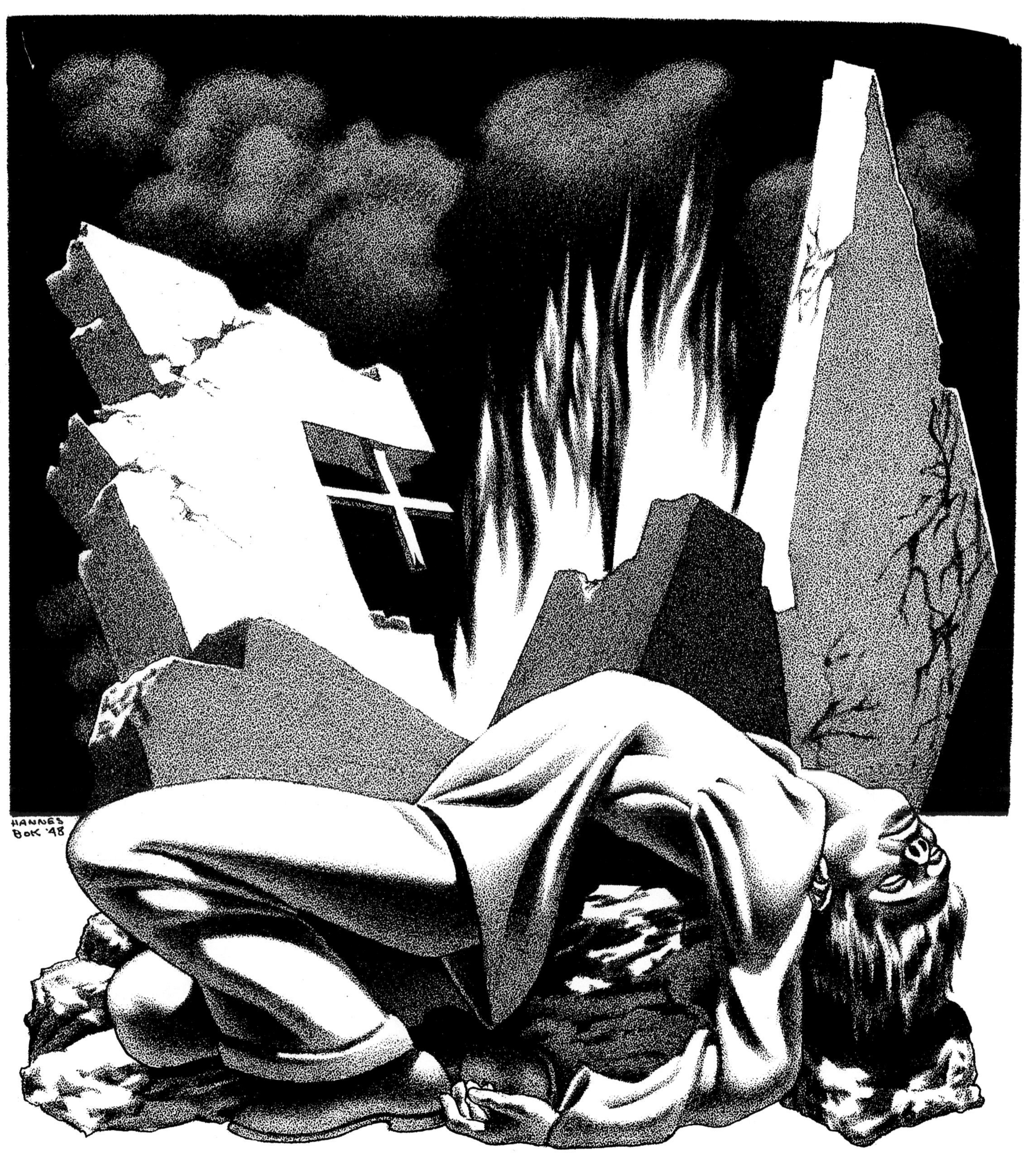

Illustration for "The Earth Killers" by A. E. Van Vogt, 1949.

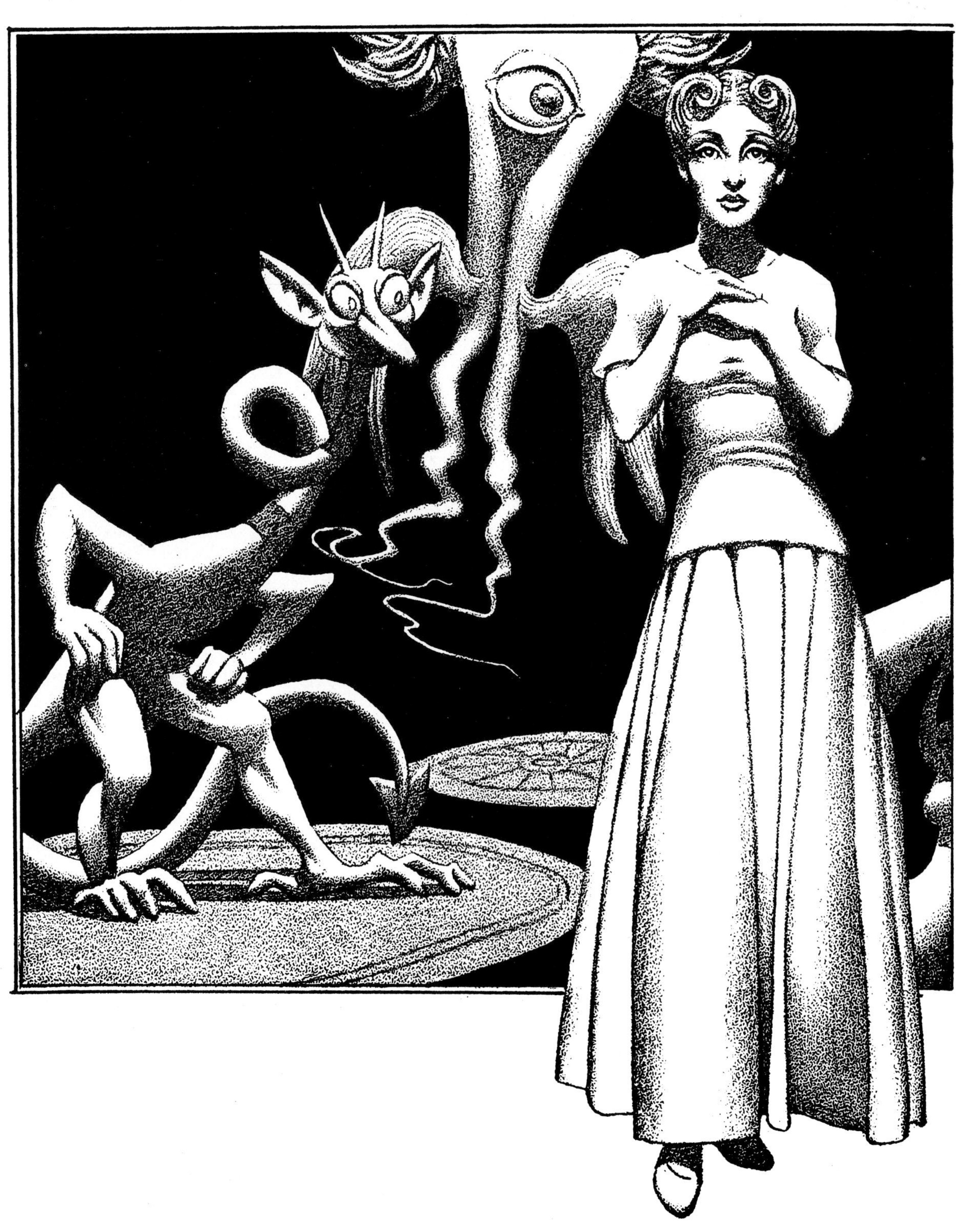

Black and white illustration

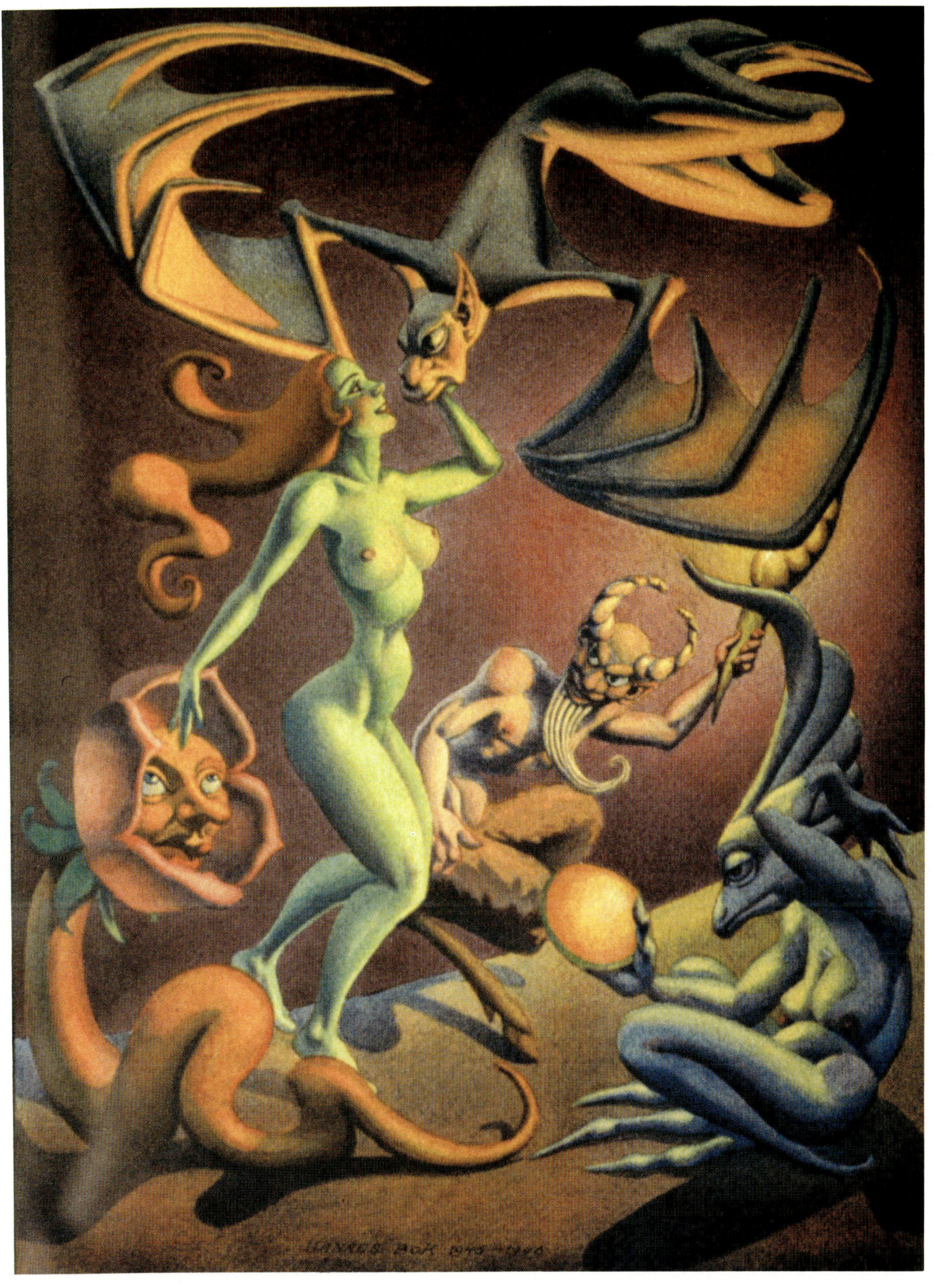

From the collection of Sig Wahrman.

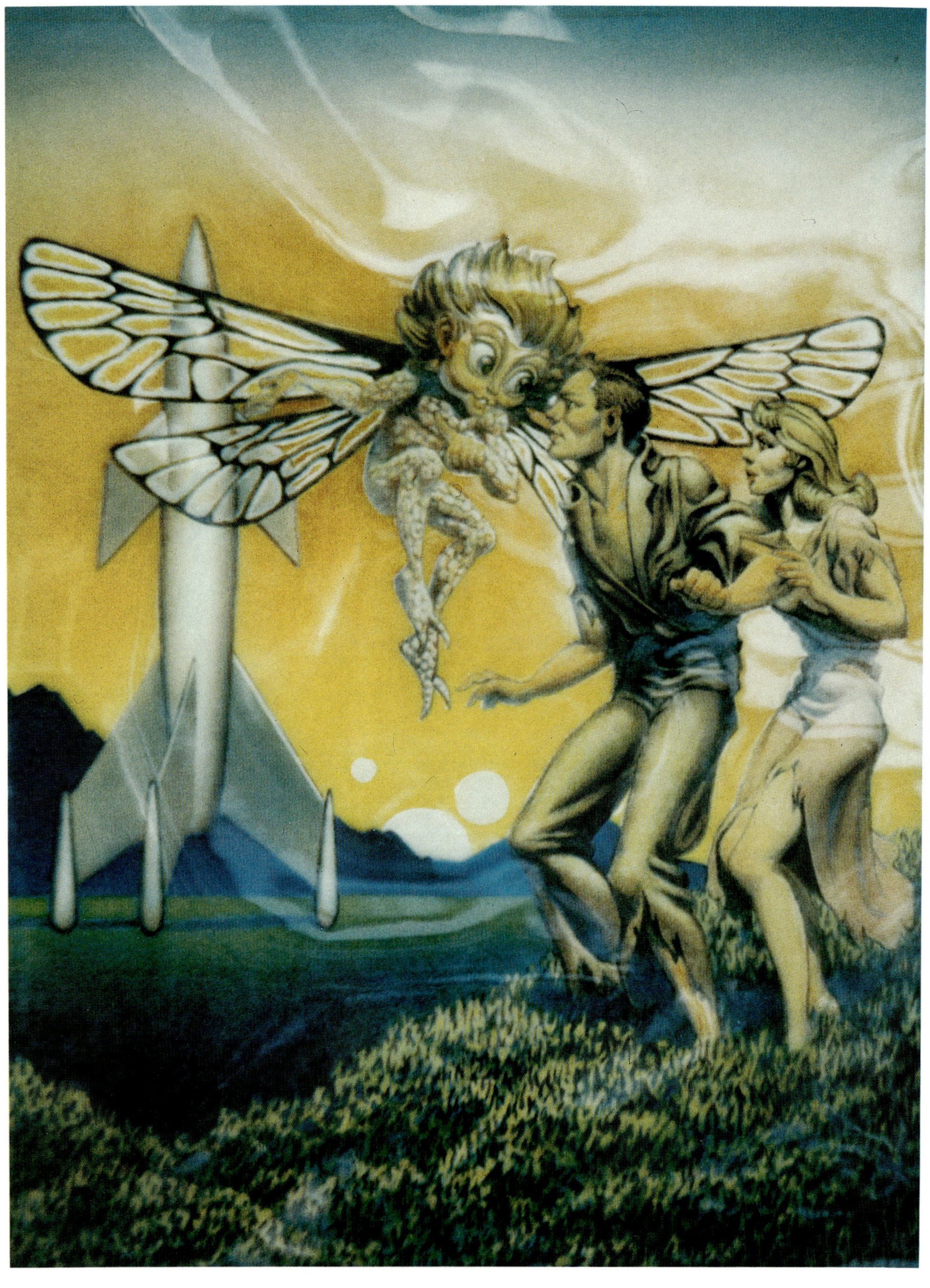

From the collection of Stephen D. Korshak.

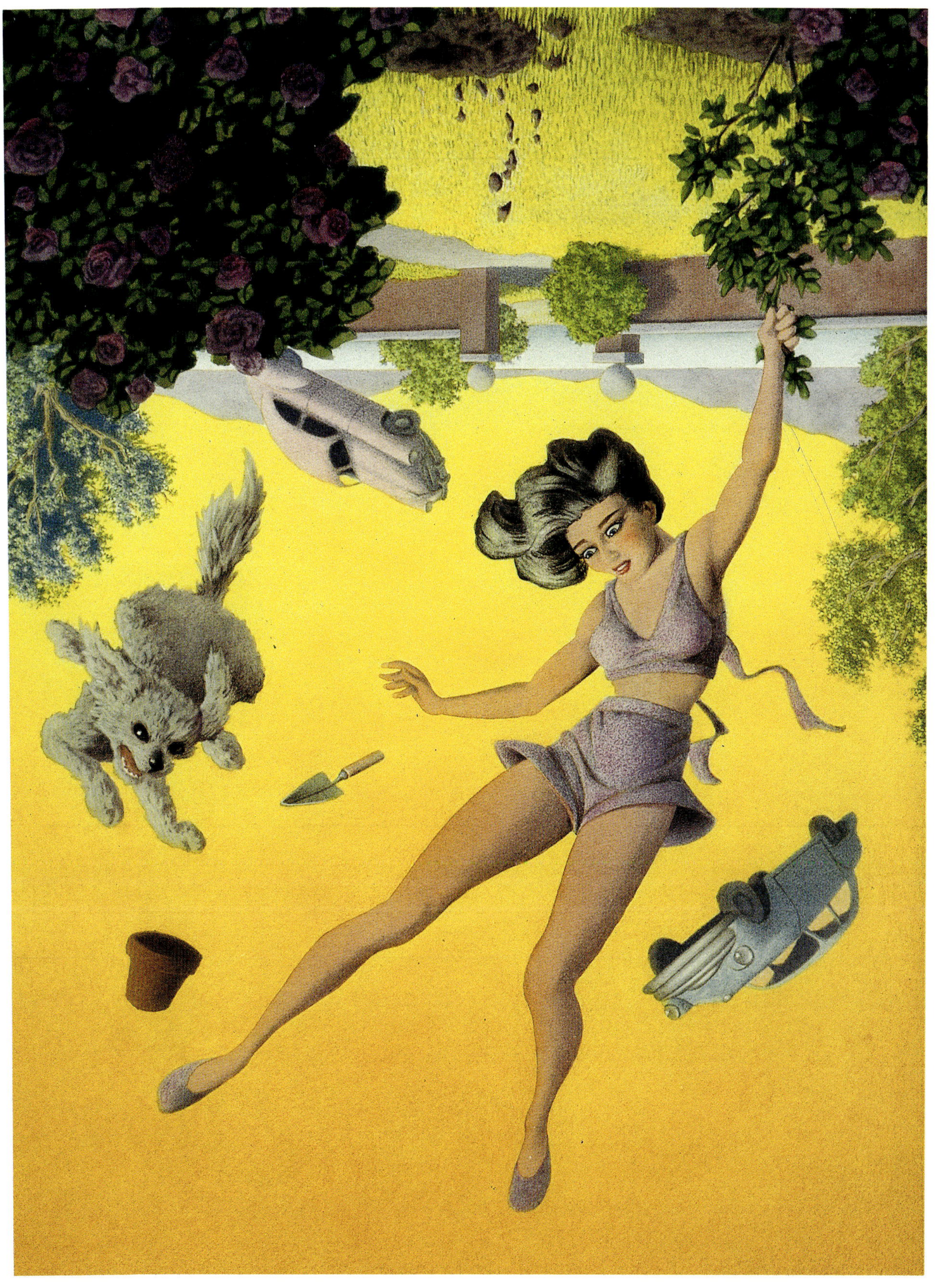

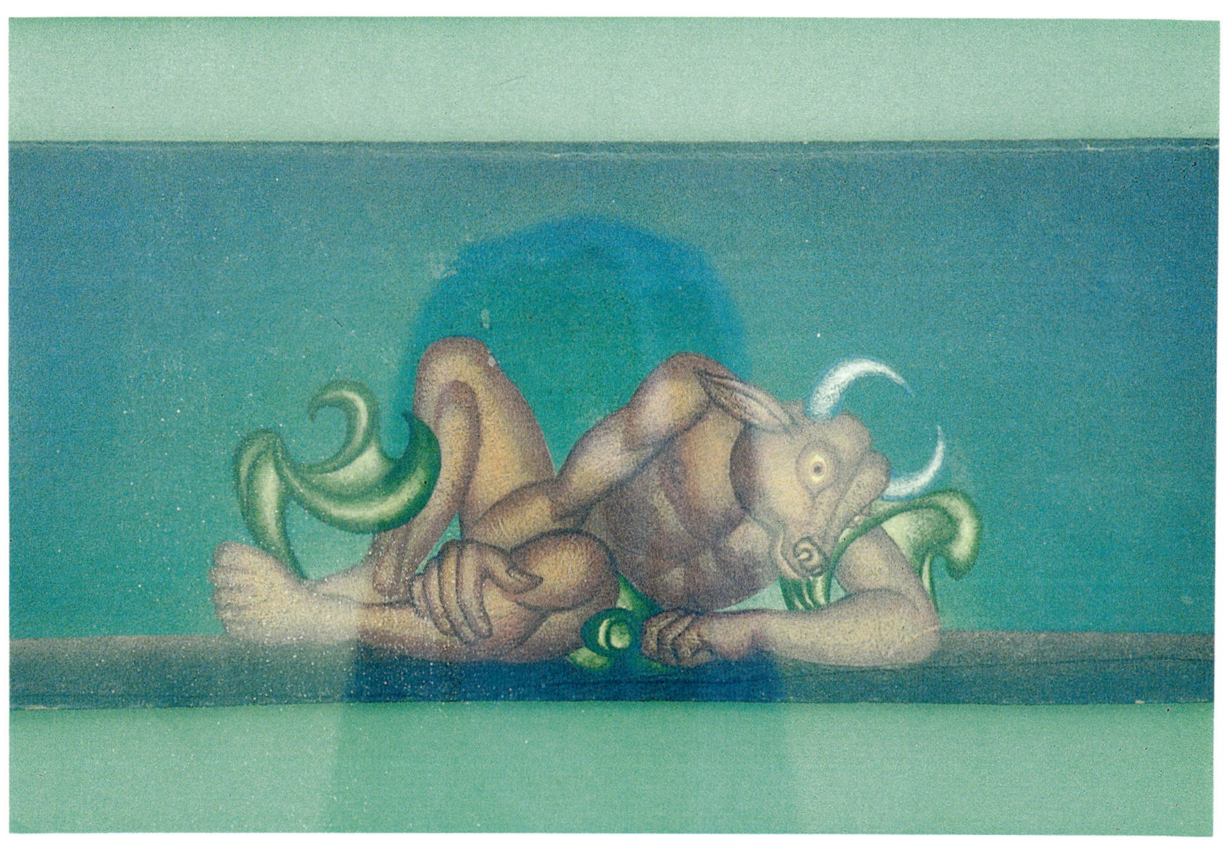

From the collection of Sig Wahrman.

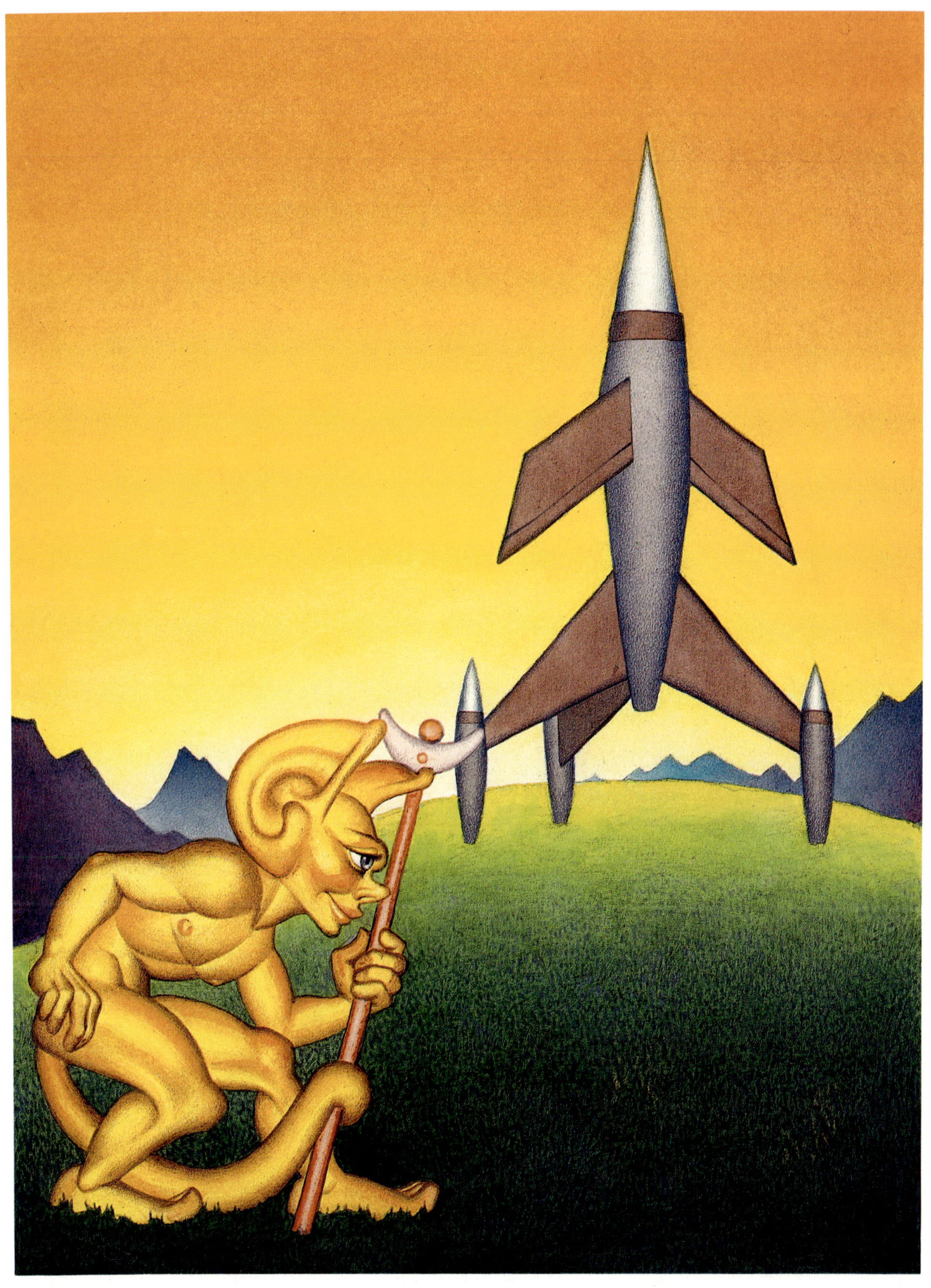

From the collection of Richard Kelly.

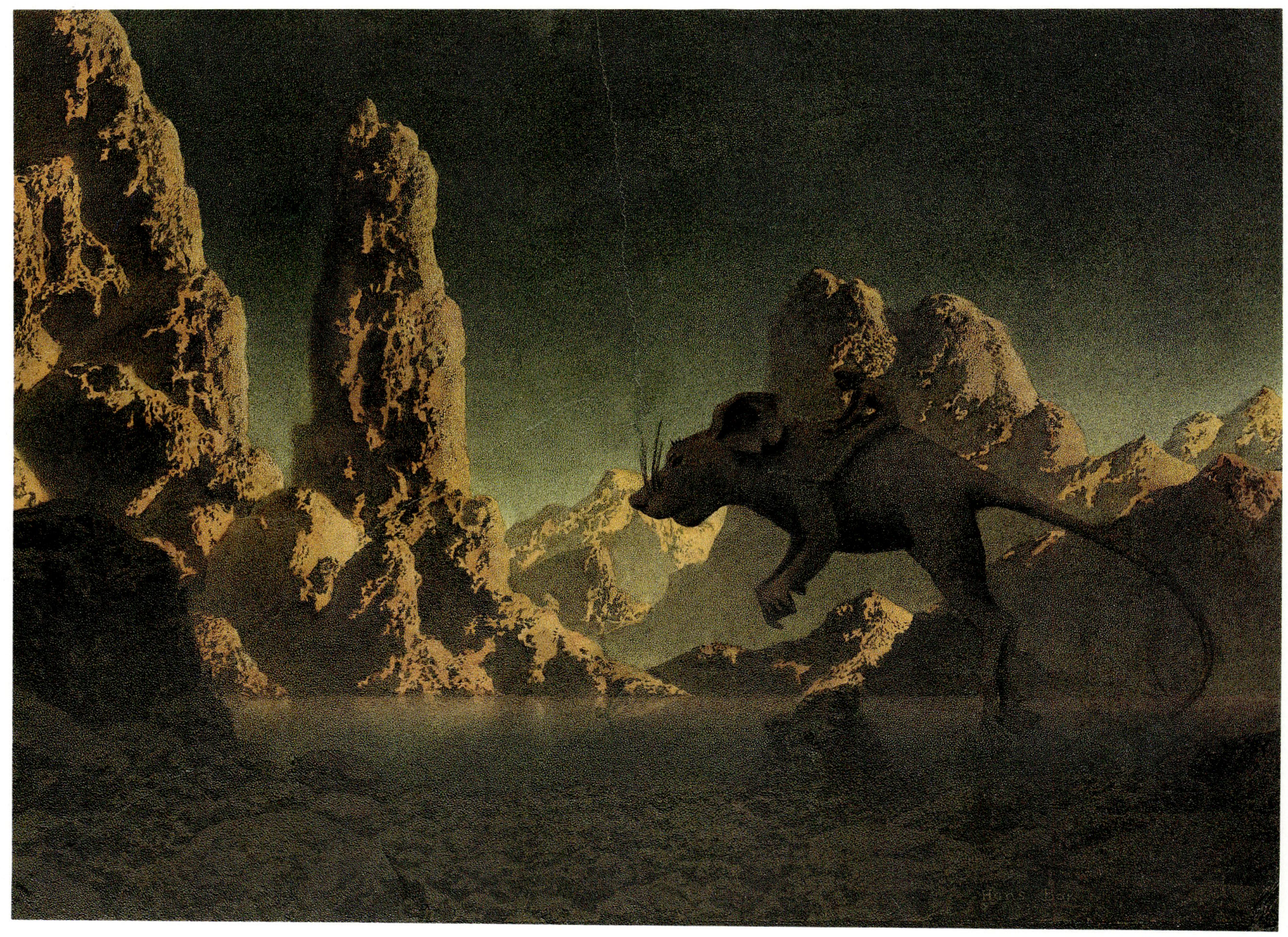

From the collection of Richard Kelly.

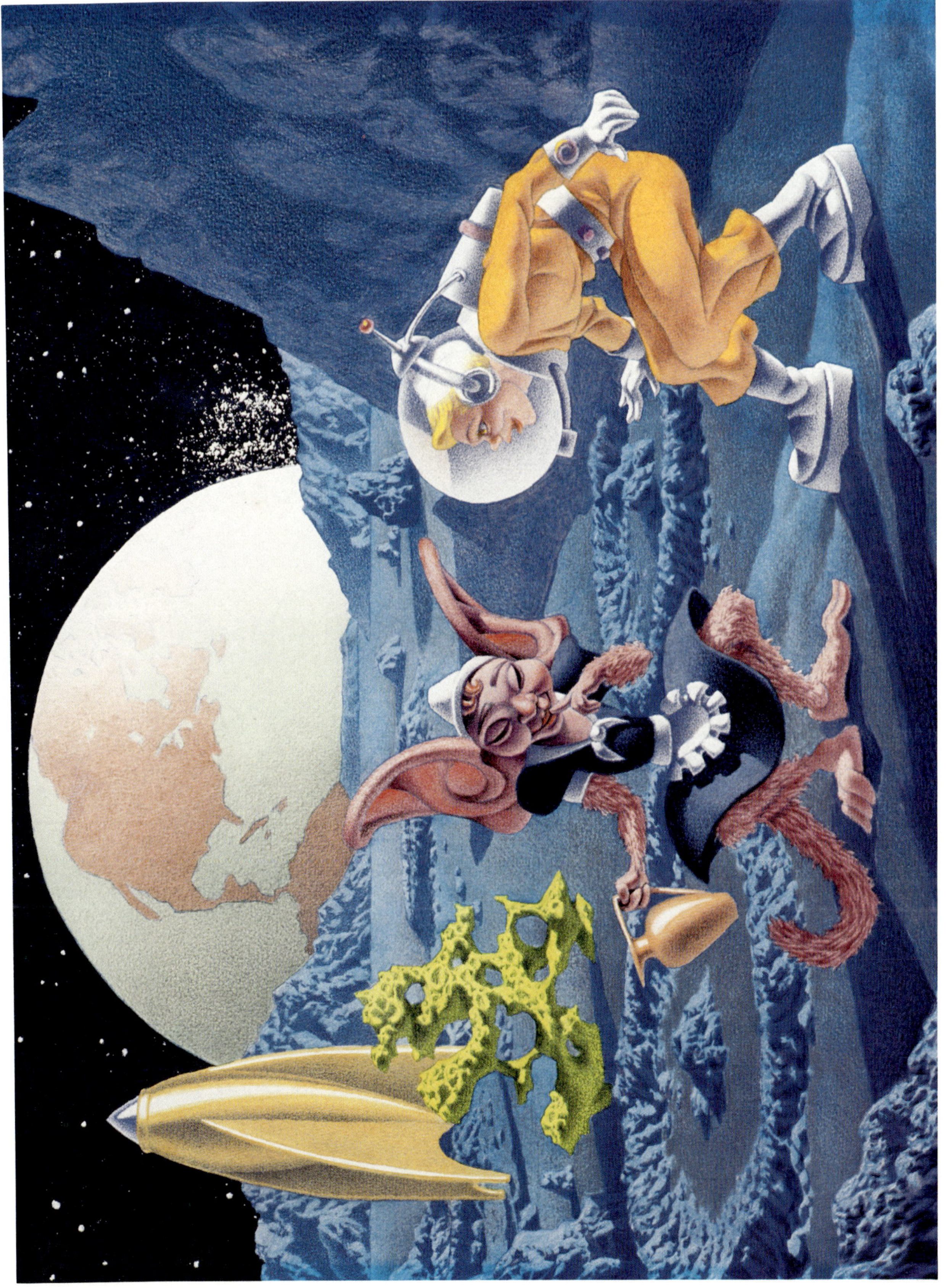

39

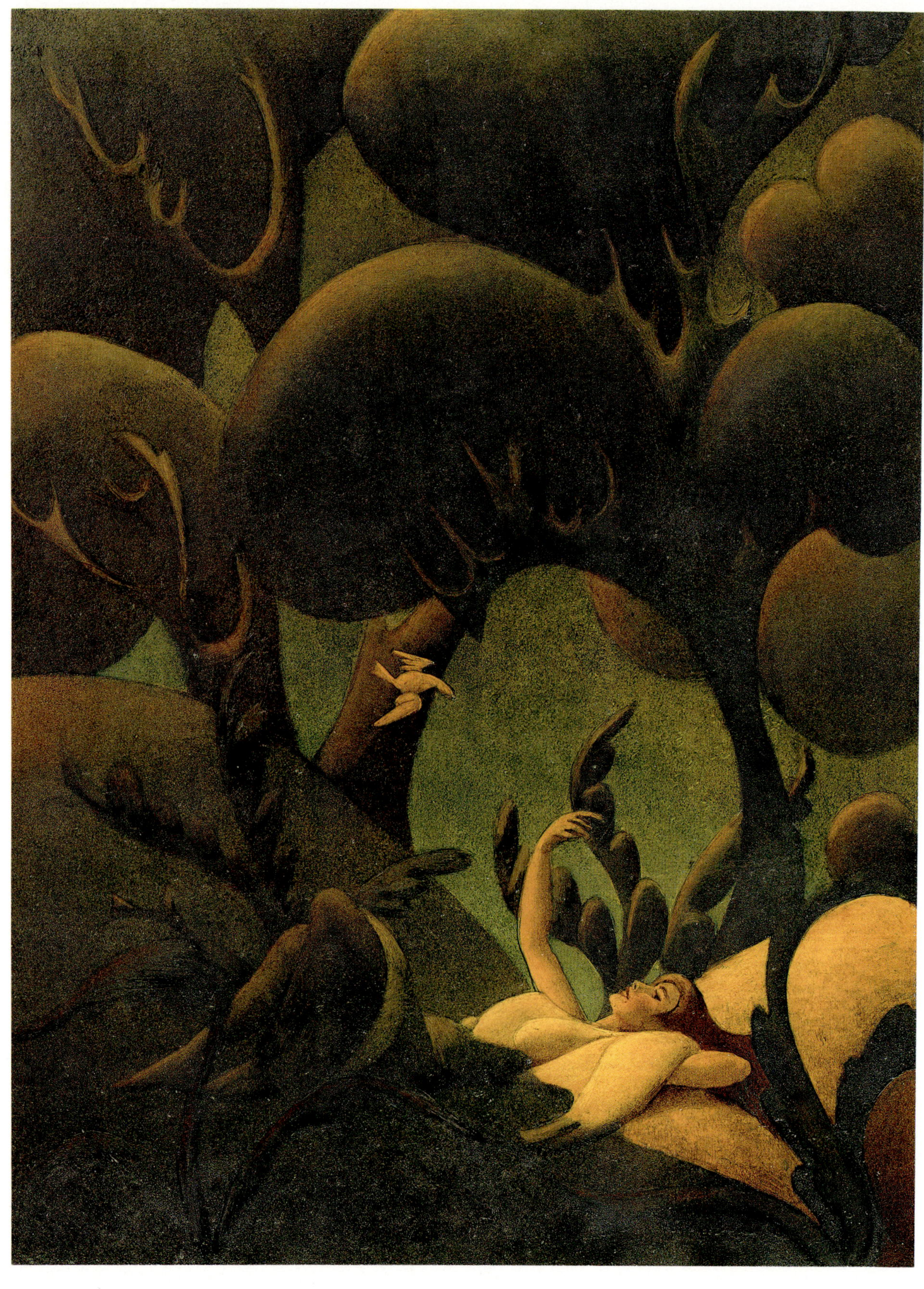

From the collection of Richard Kelly.

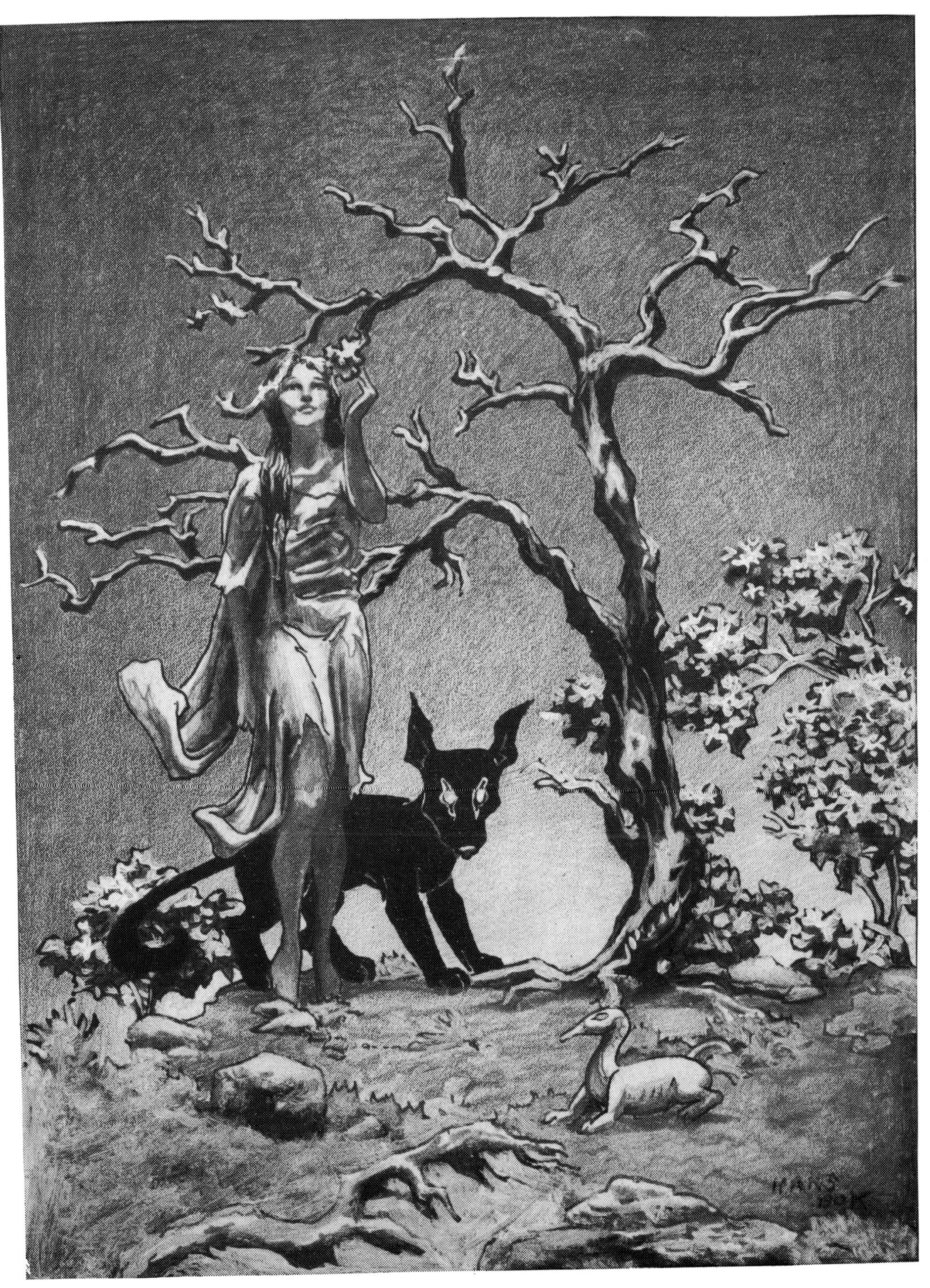

Illustration for "The Last Leaf," 1936.

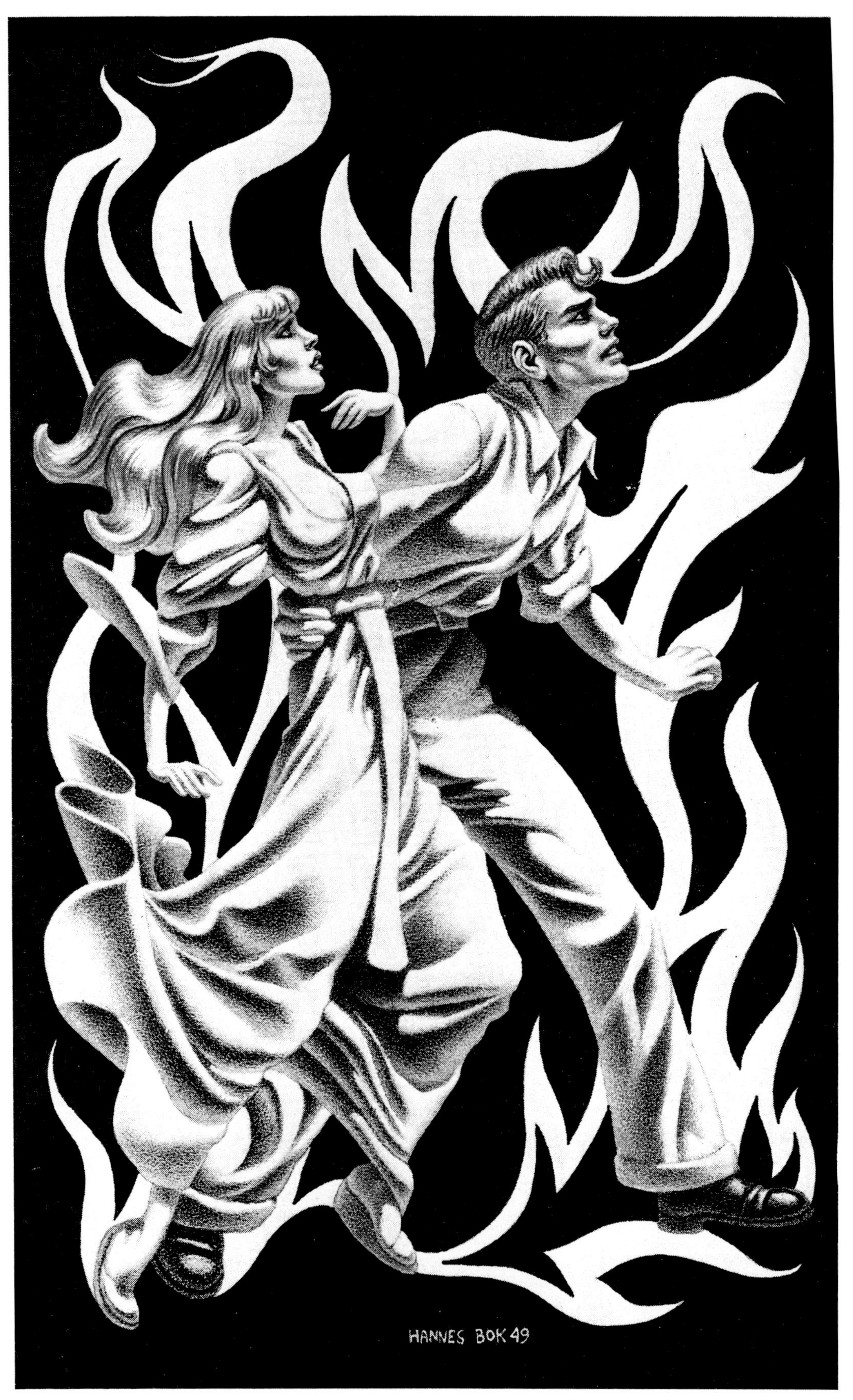

Illustration for "The Spot of Life" by Austin Hall, 1951.

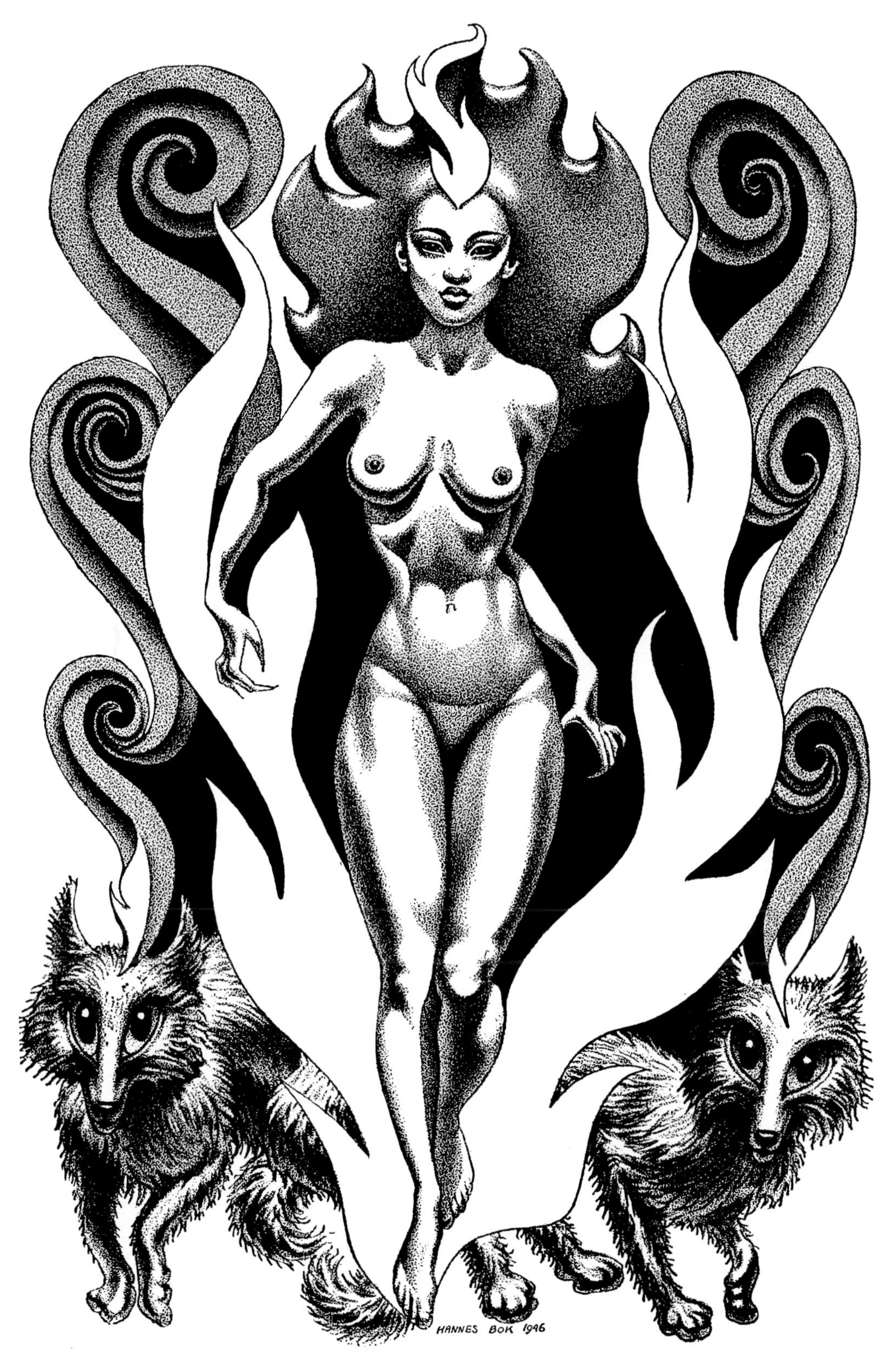

Illustration for "The Fox Woman and the Blue Pagoda," by A. Merritt & Hannes Bok, 1946.

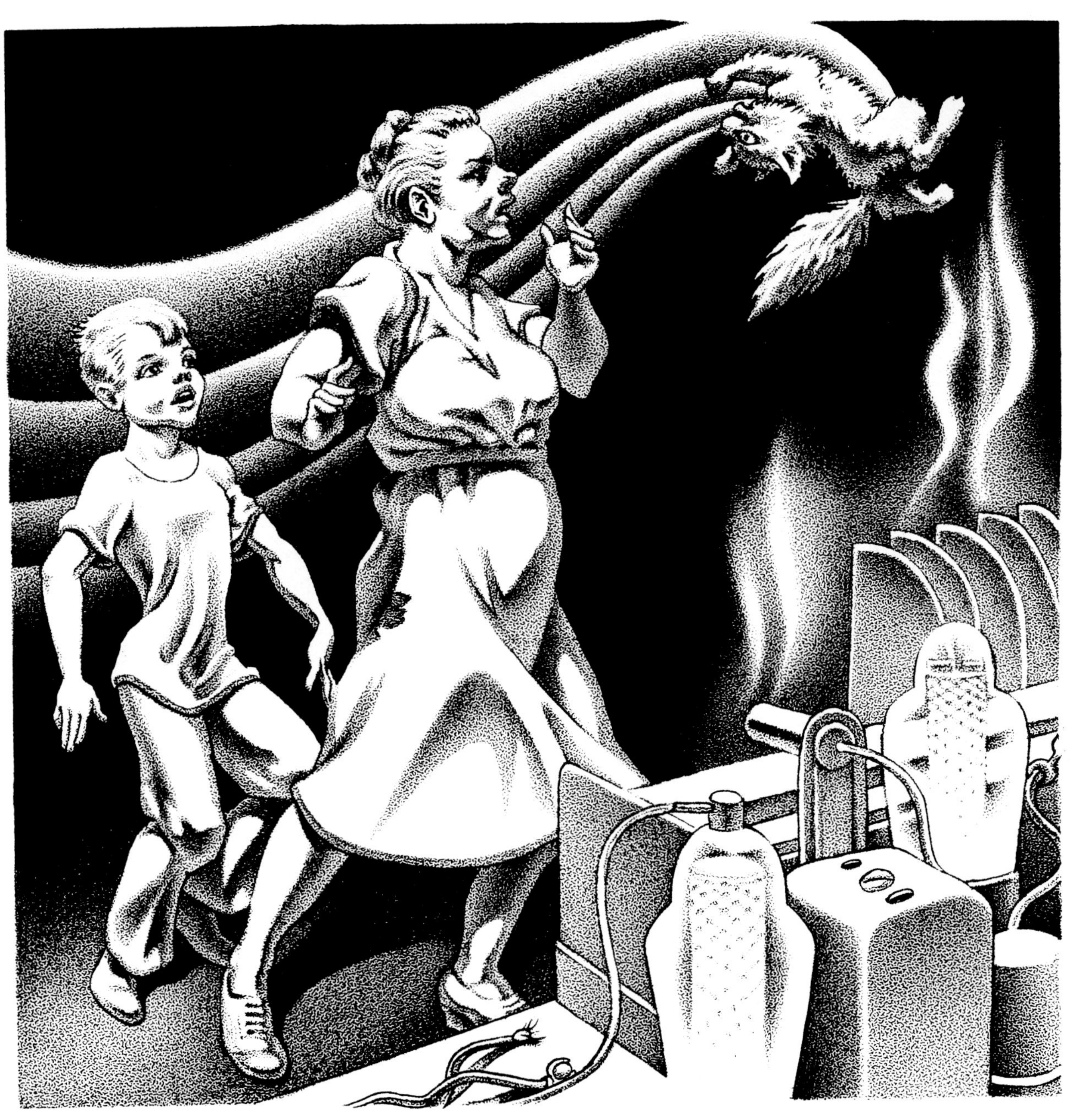

Black and white illustration

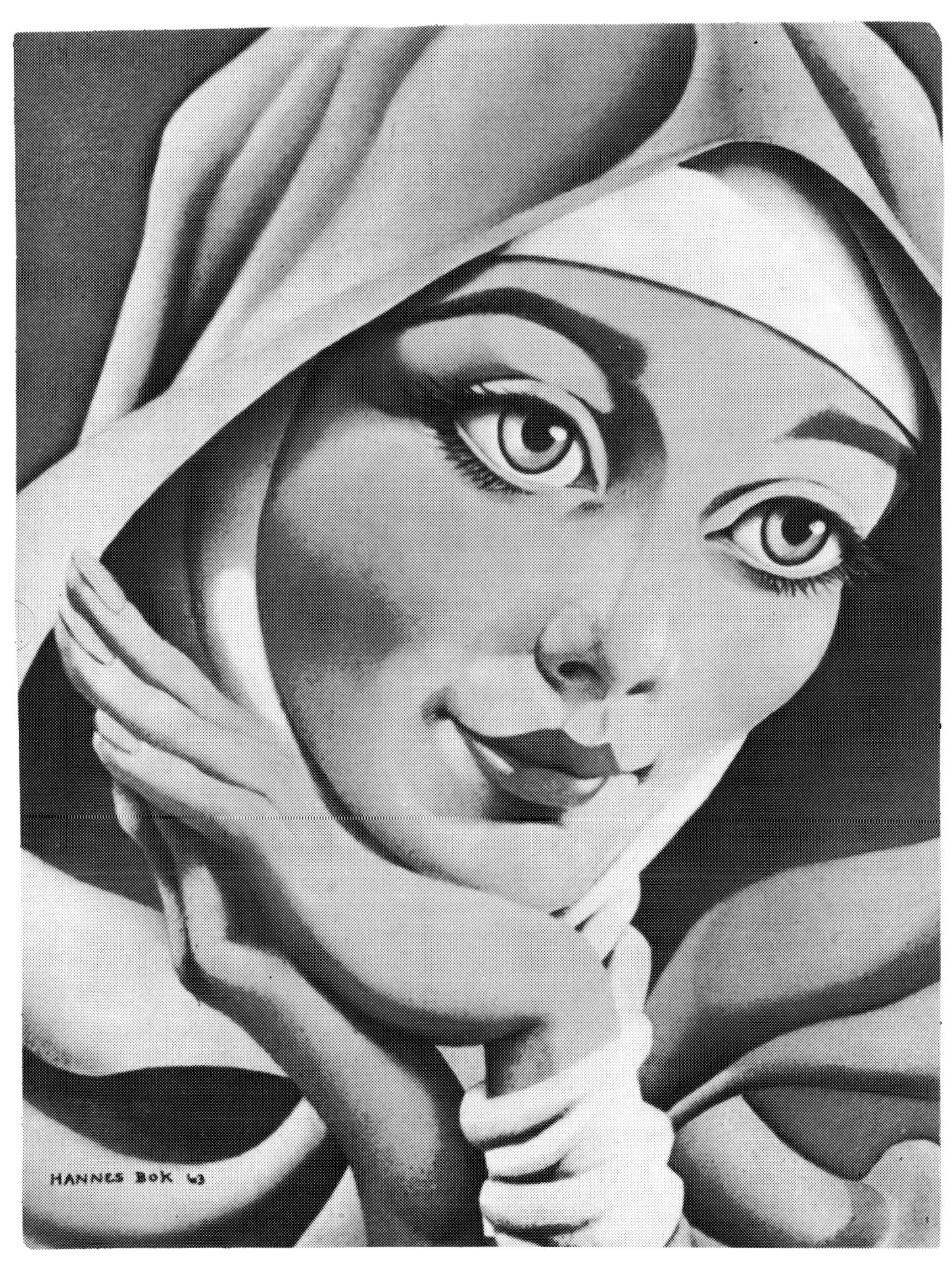

Black and white illustration

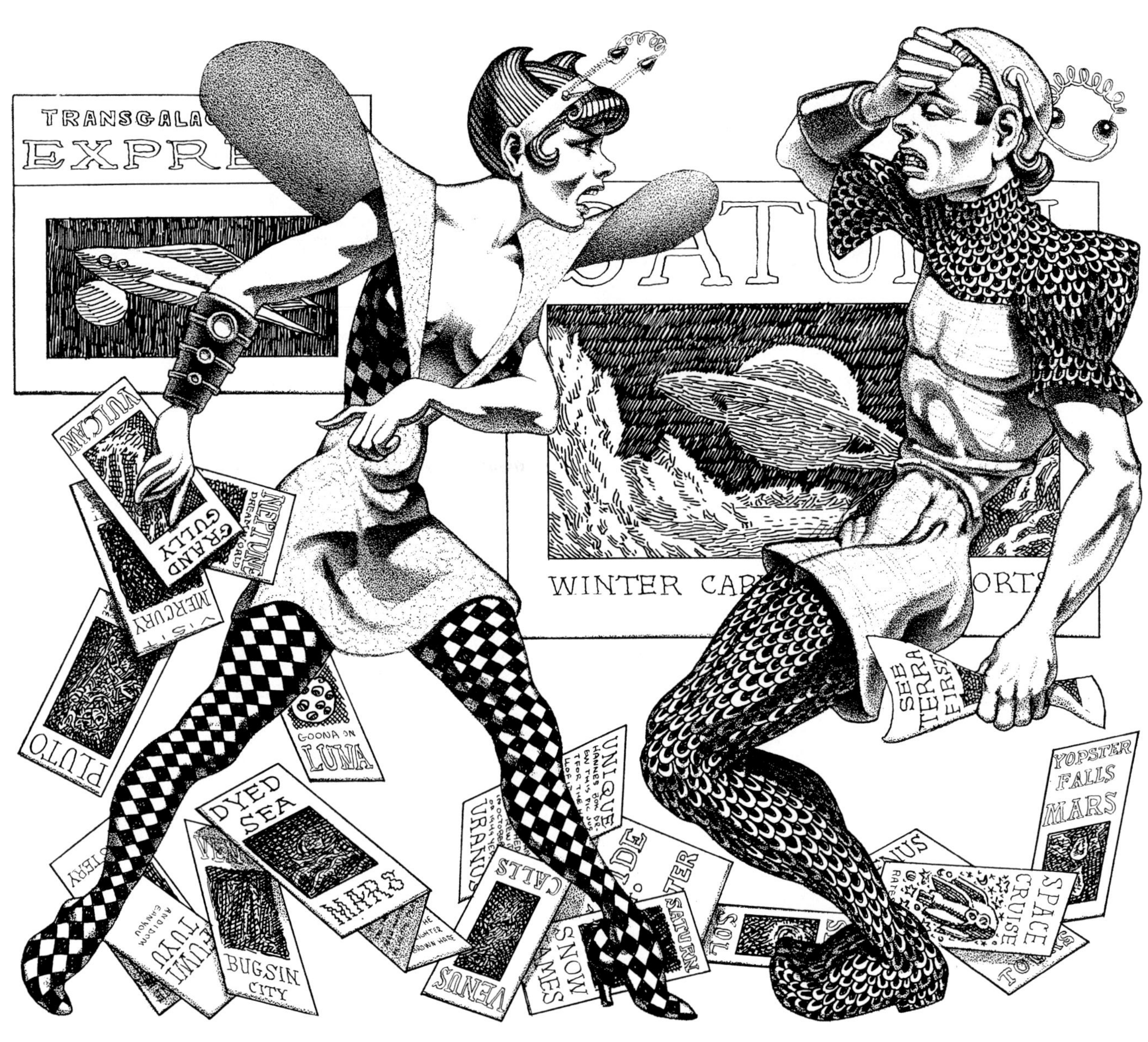

Illustration for "Vacation-Time Blues," 1949.

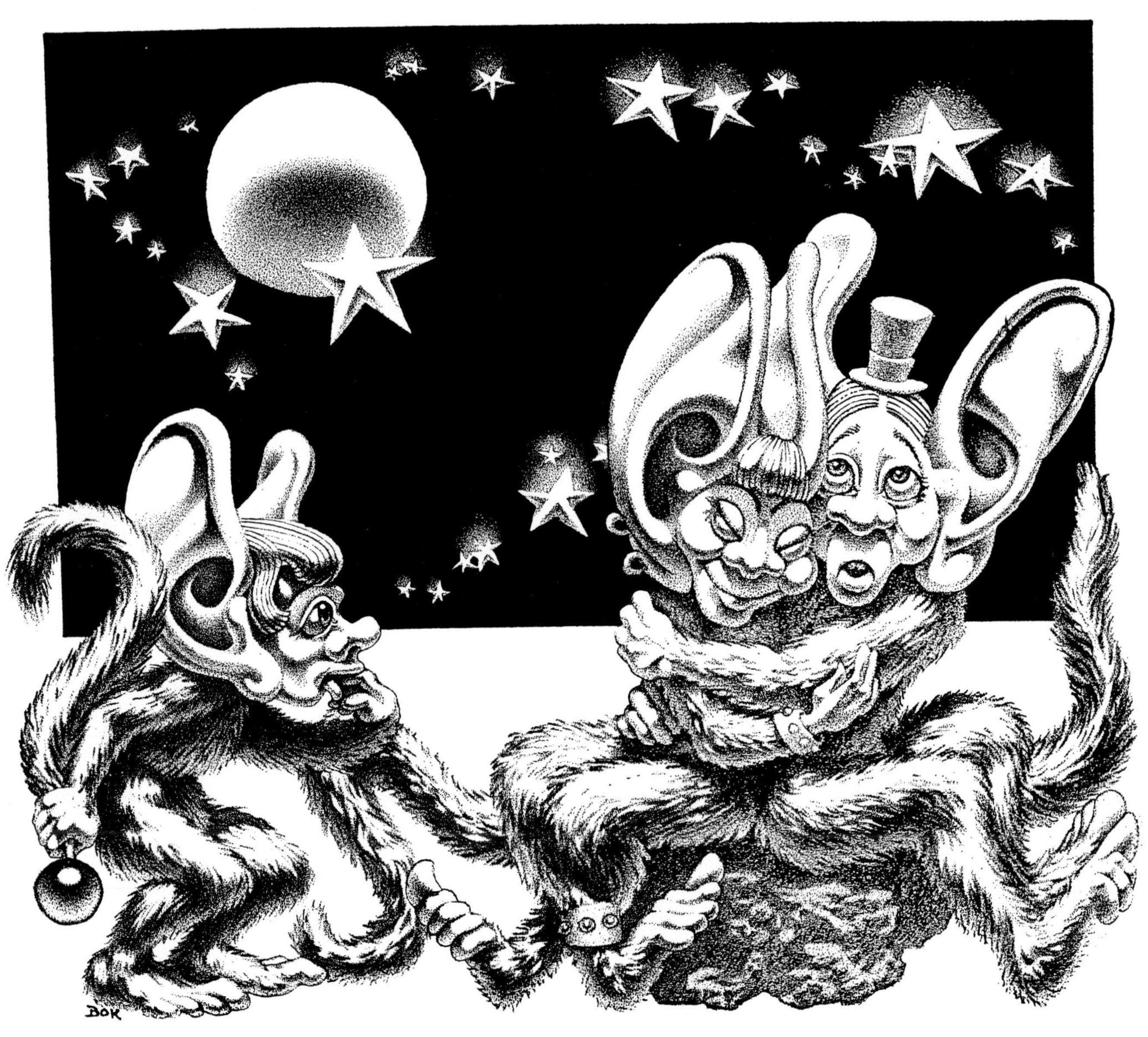

Illustration for "Gizzelstein Honeymoon," 1948.

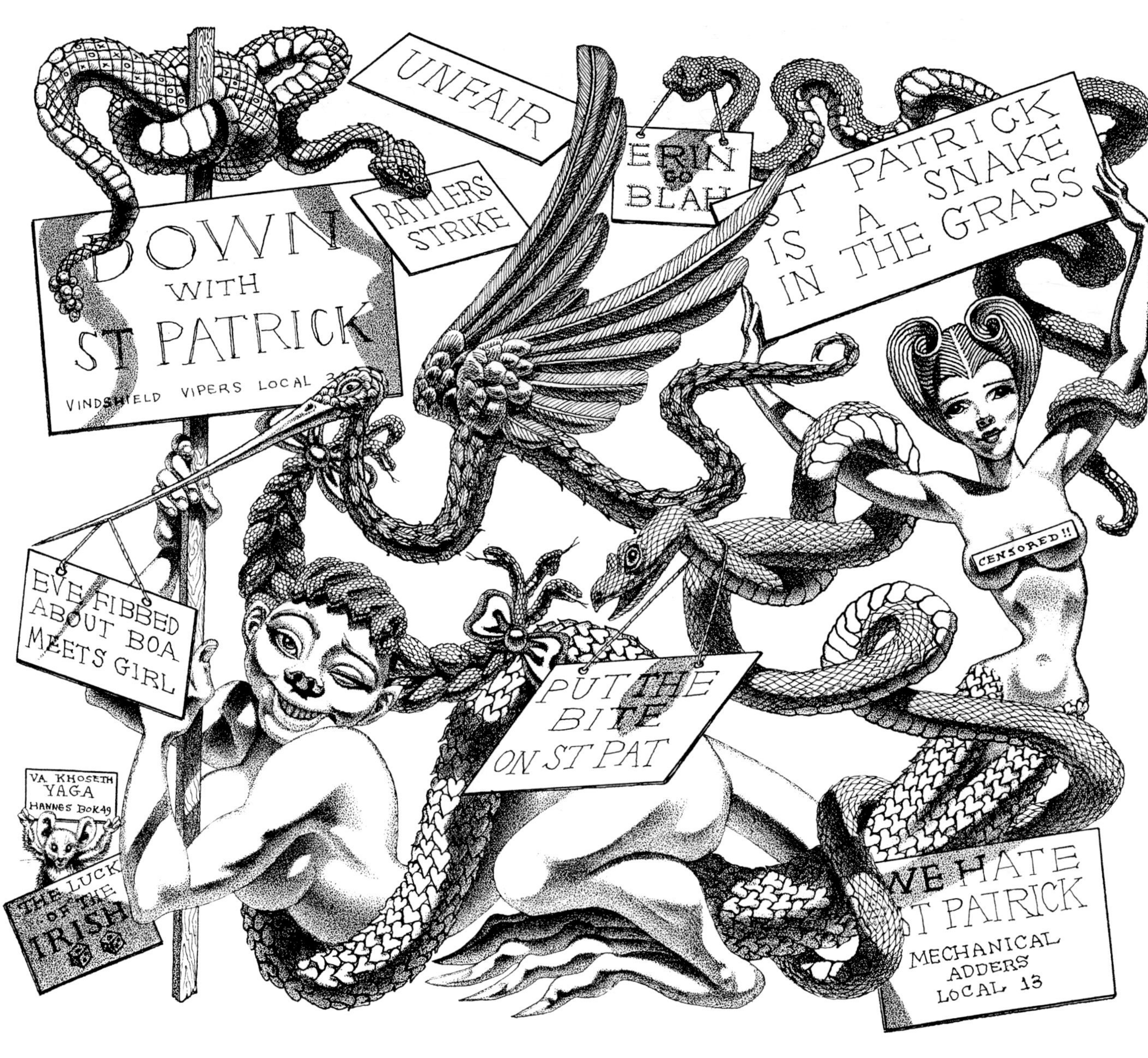

Illustration for "Swearing O' The Green," 1949.

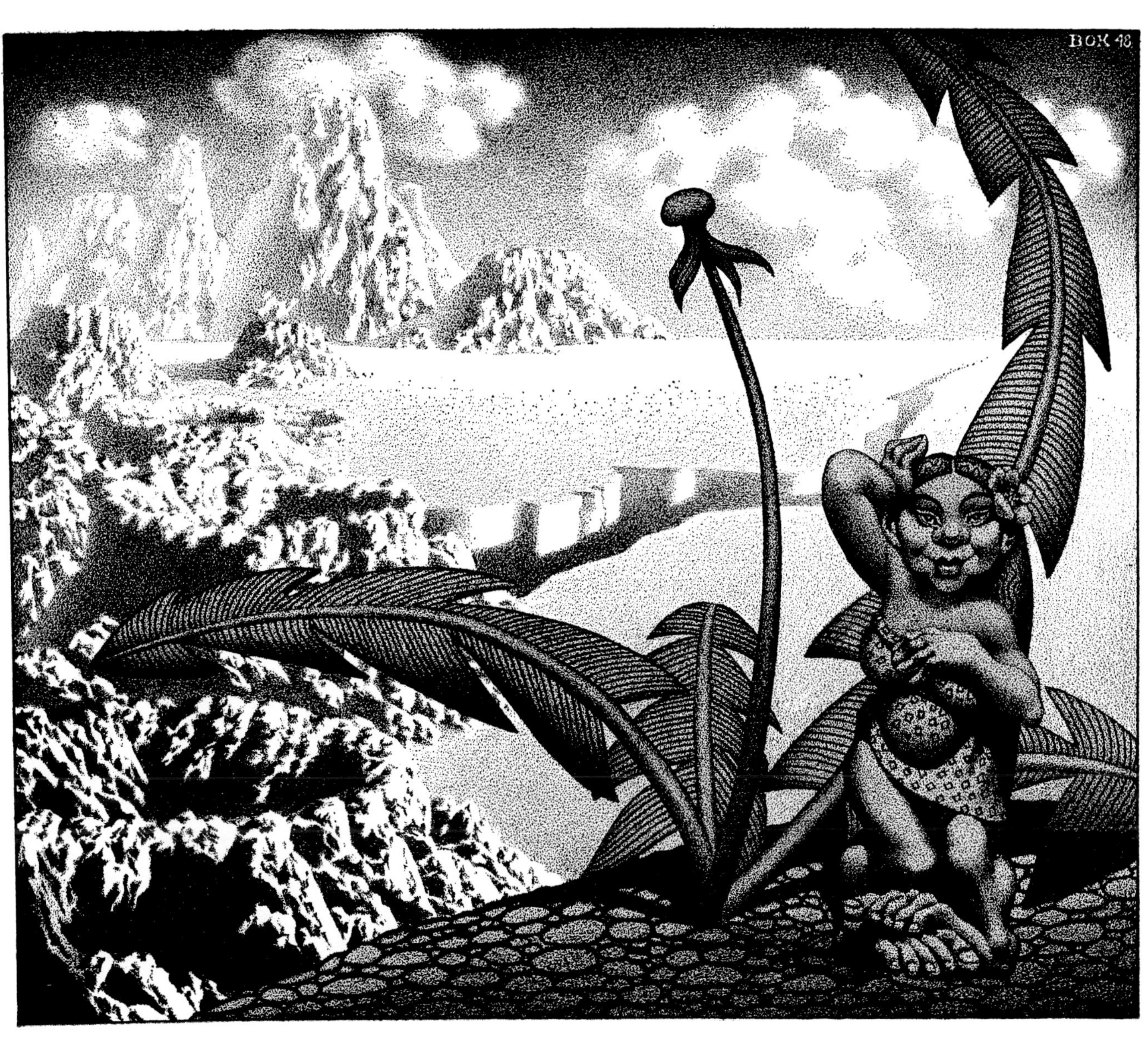

Illustration for "Welcome to Mercury," 1948.

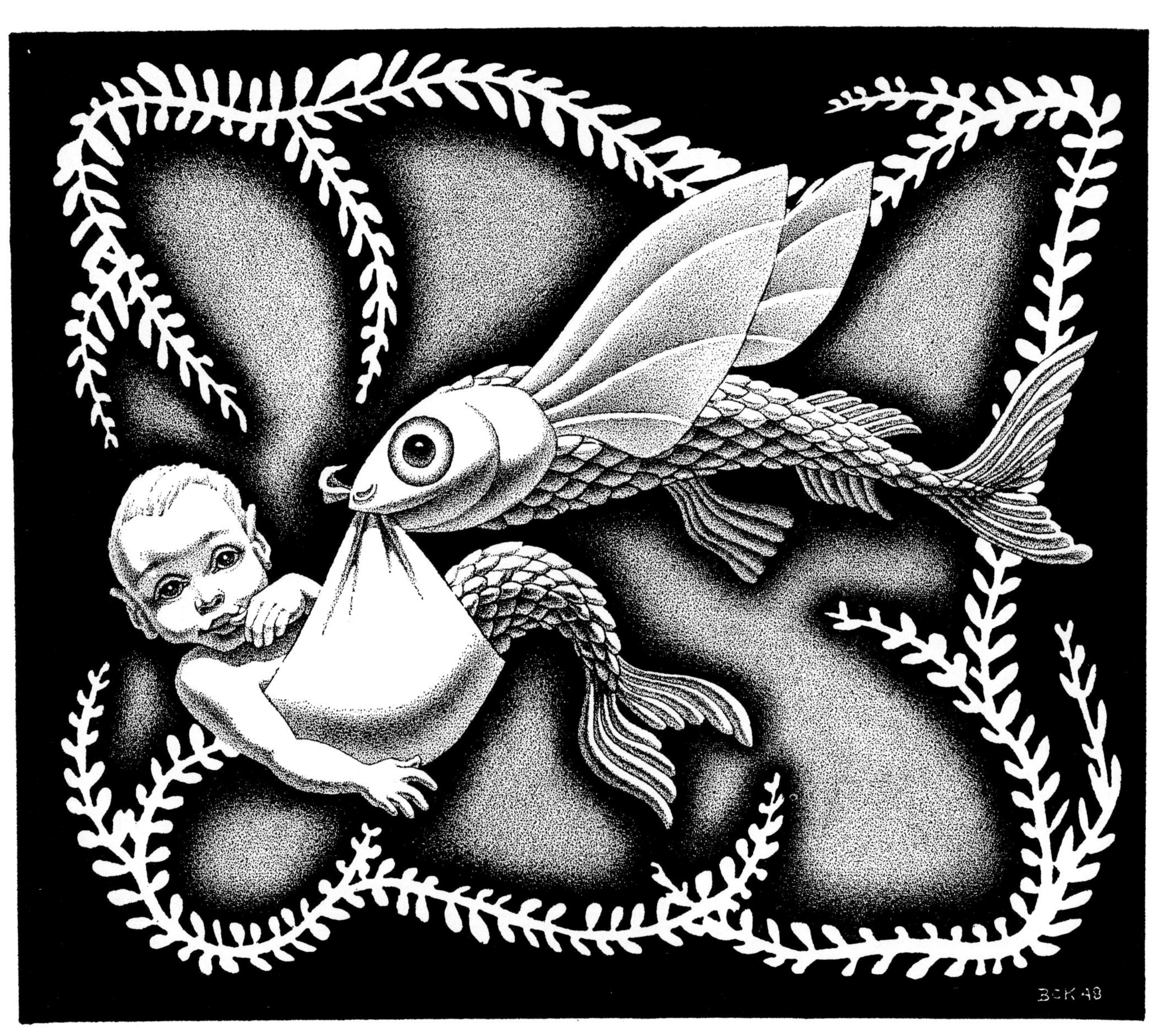

Illustration for "The Stork Fish," 1948.

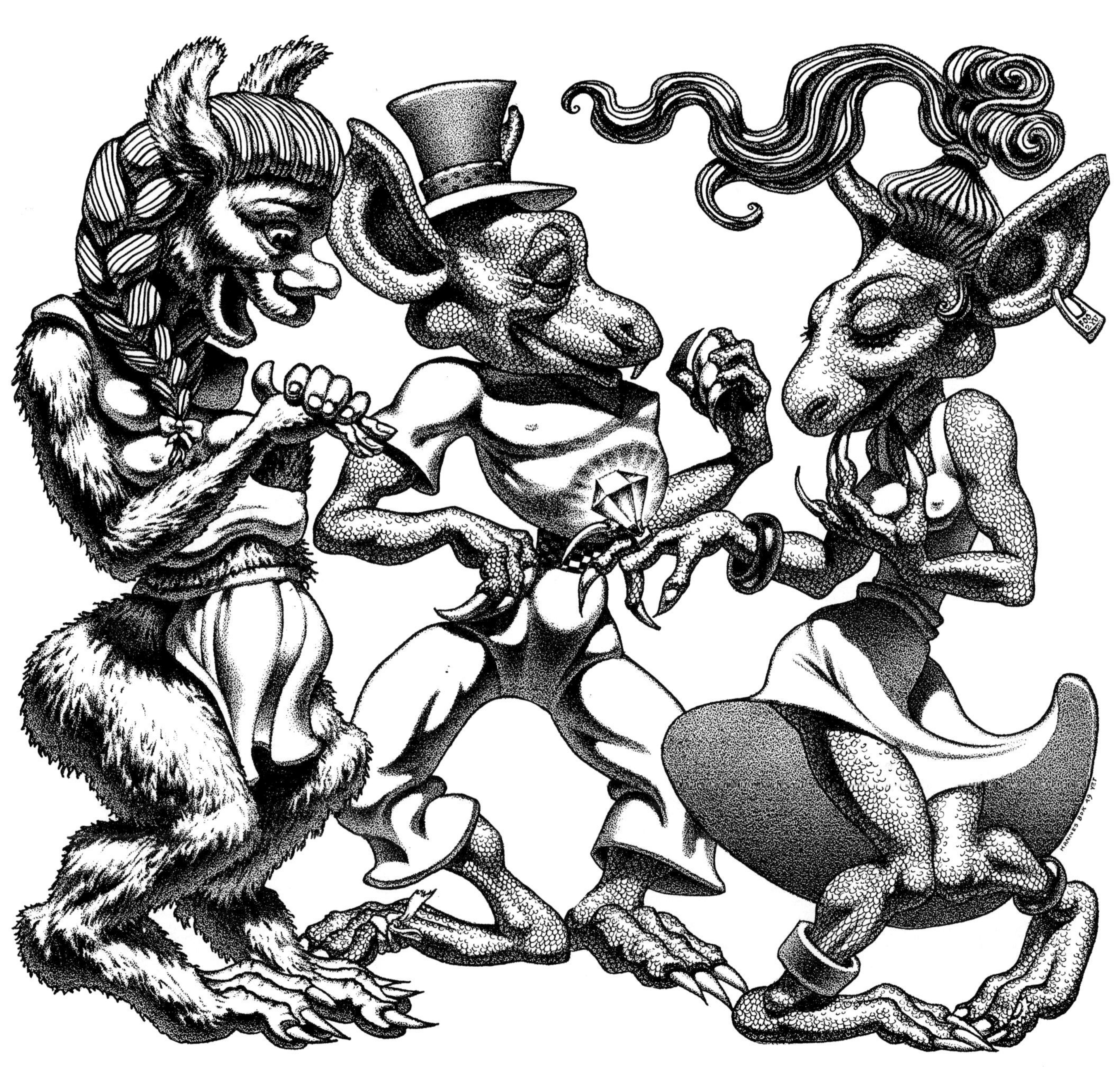

Illustration for "She's Lovely, She's Engaged, She Uses Soap," 1949.

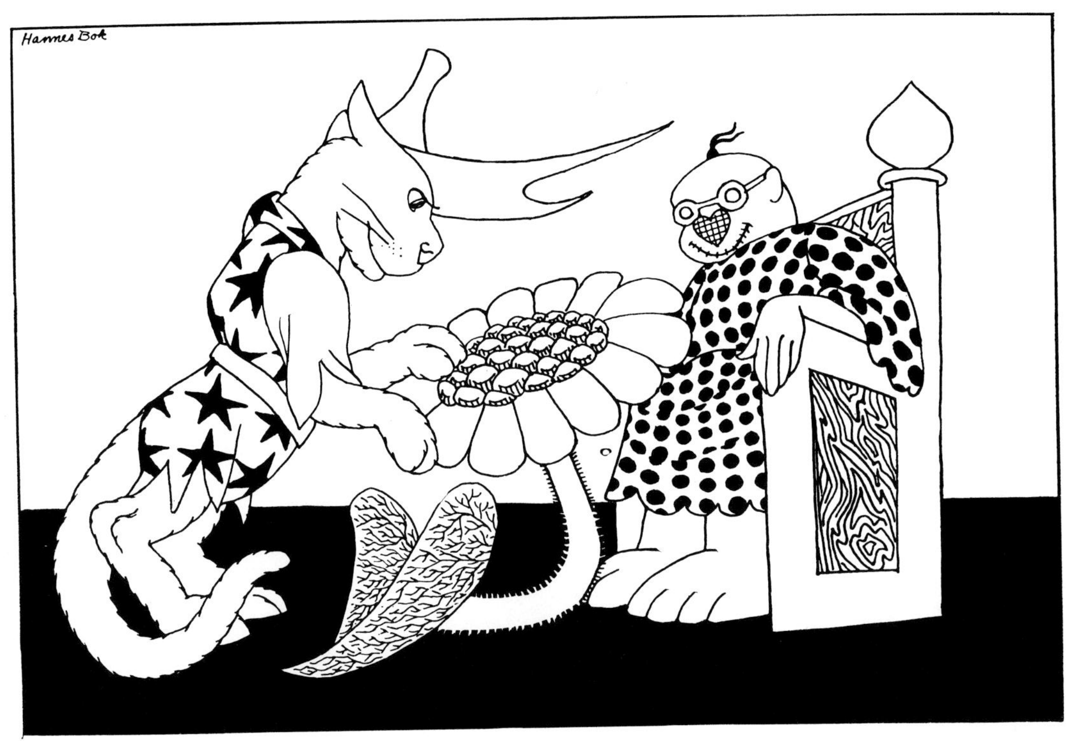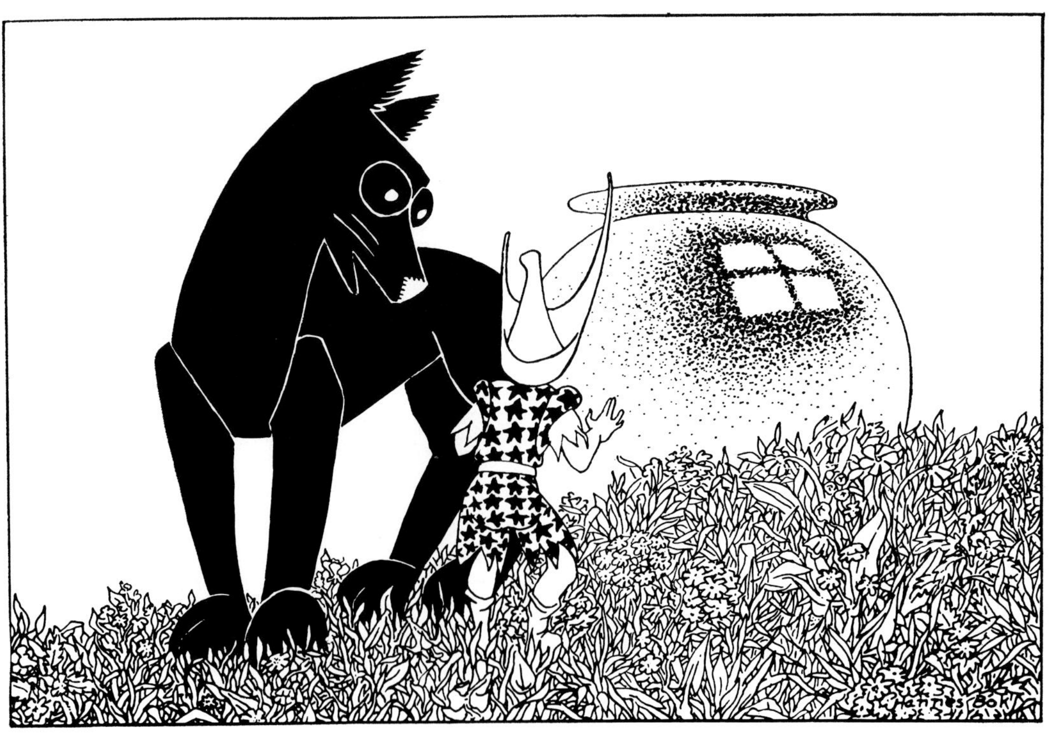

Illustration for "The Adventures of Dwinkle" by Midge Kelly, 1940.

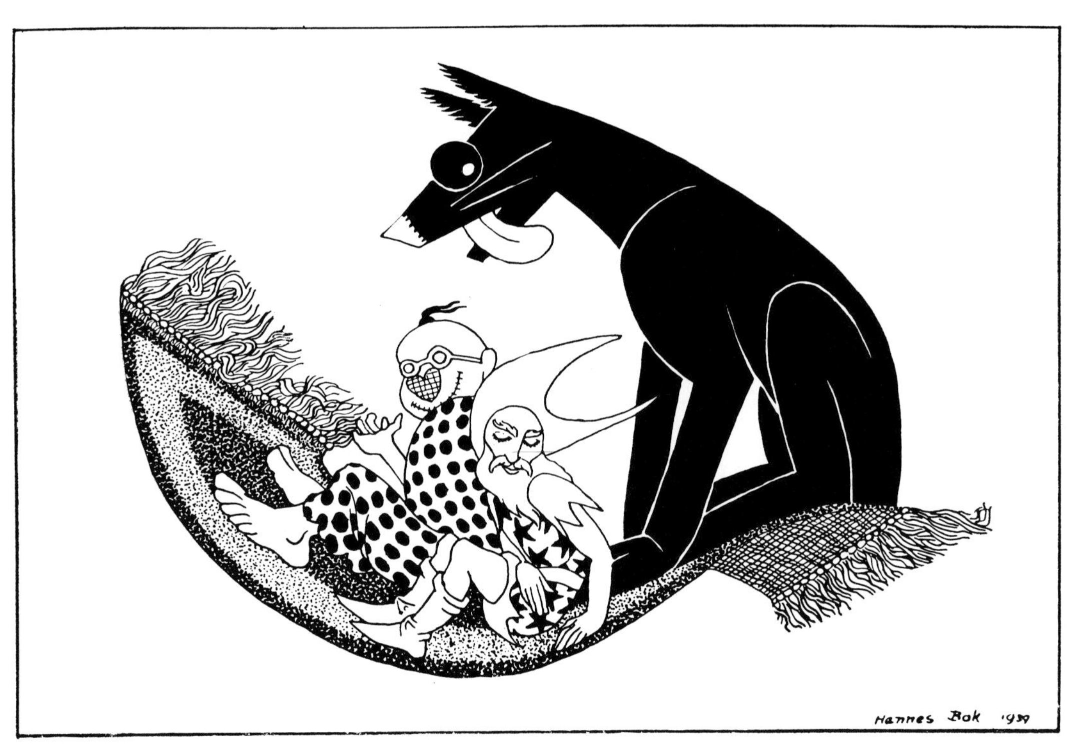

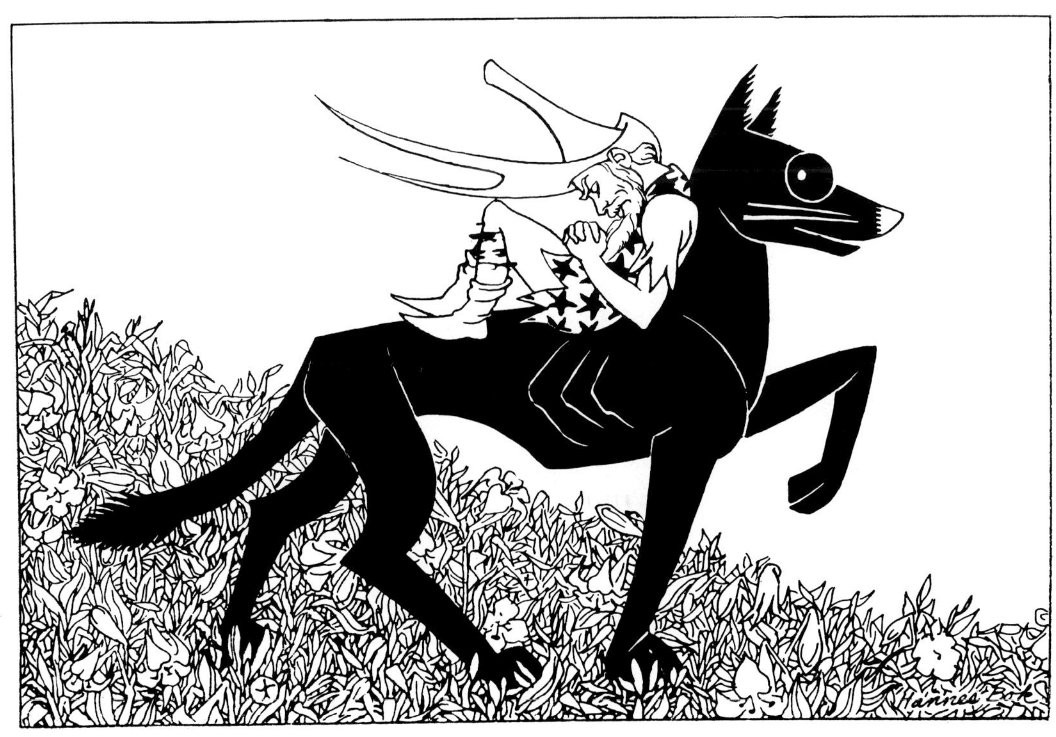

Illustration for "The Adventures of Dwinkle" by Midge Kelly, 1940.

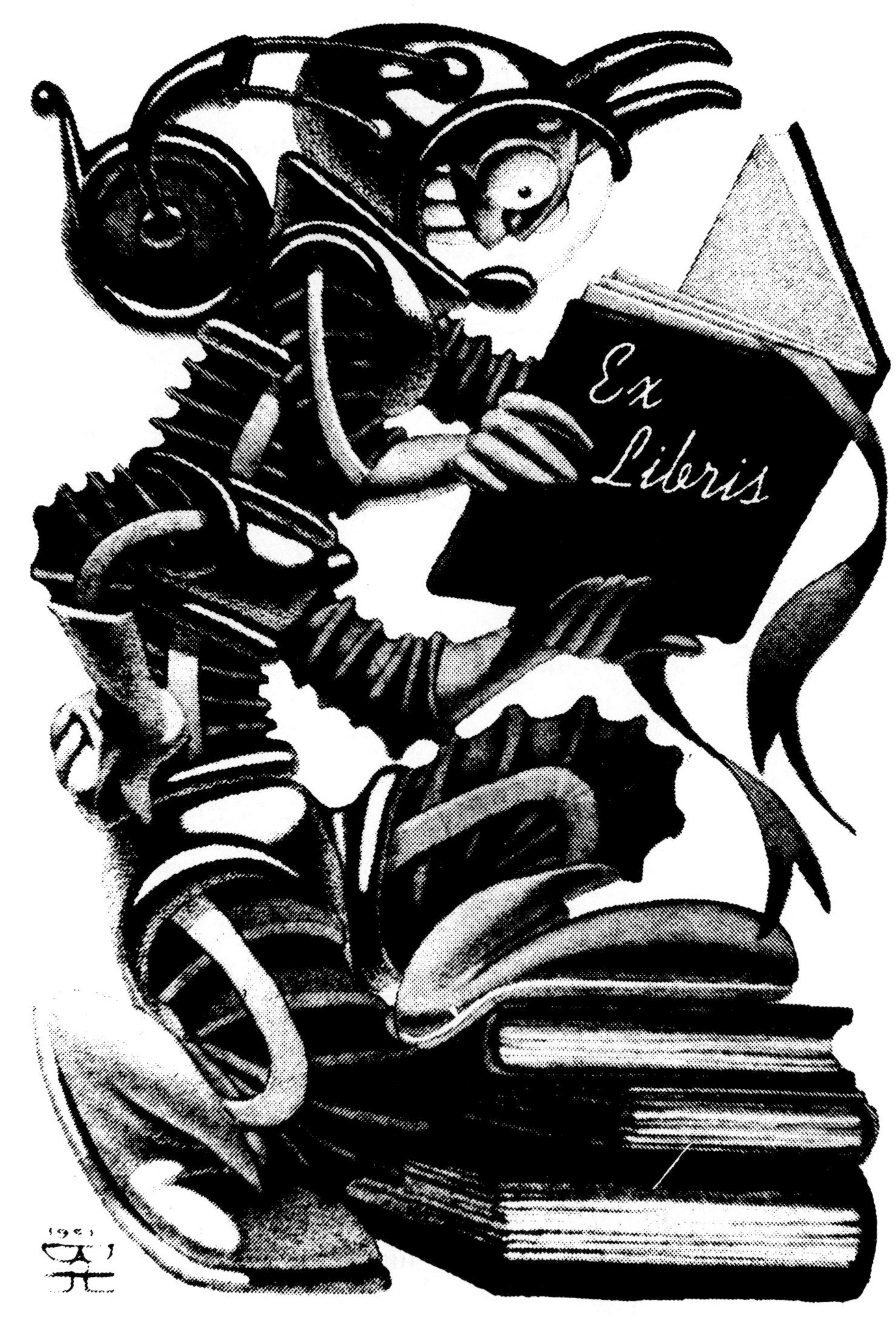

(Your Name Here)

Bookplate

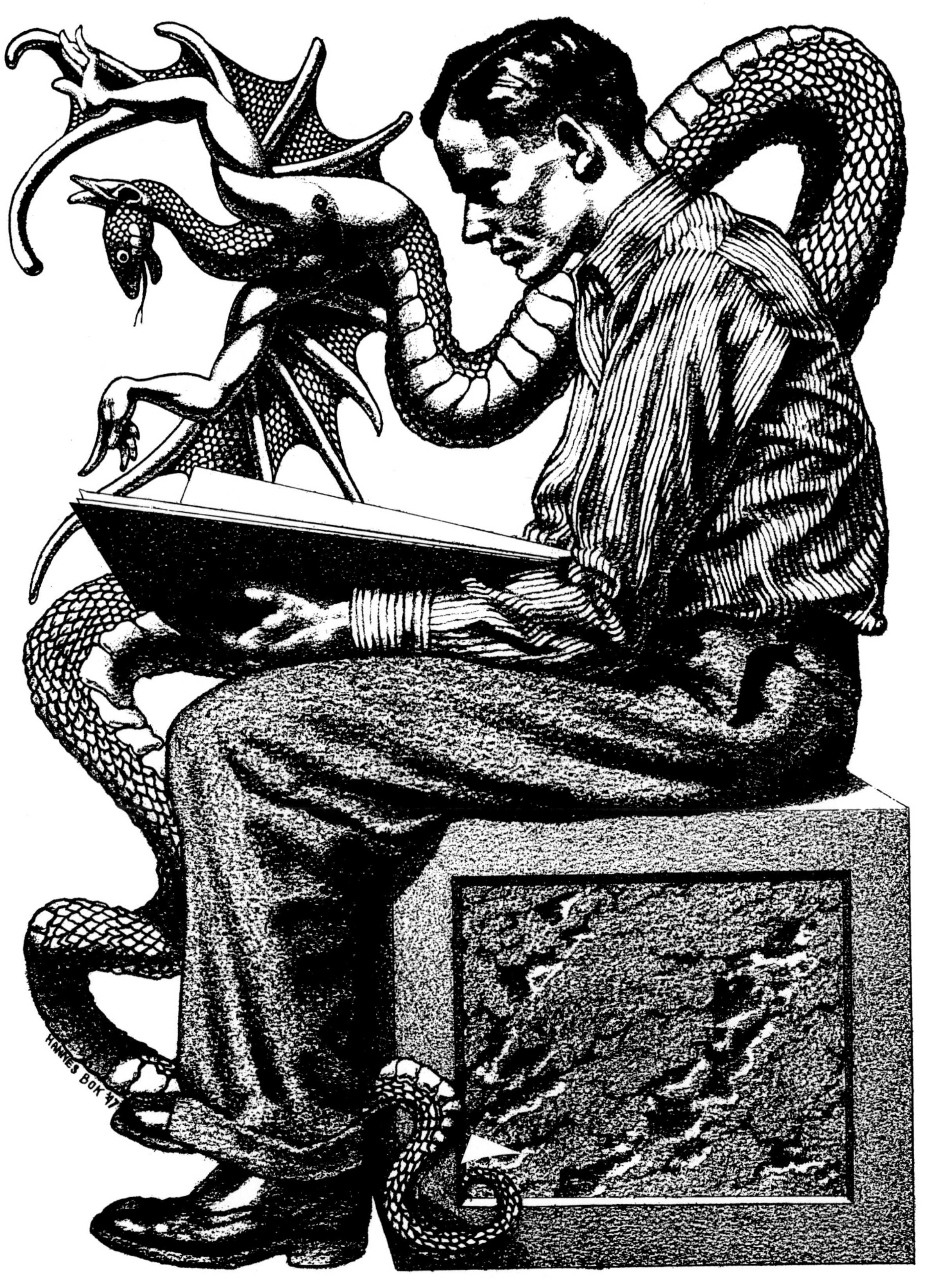

Illustration for "Portrait of Jack Grubel," 1947.

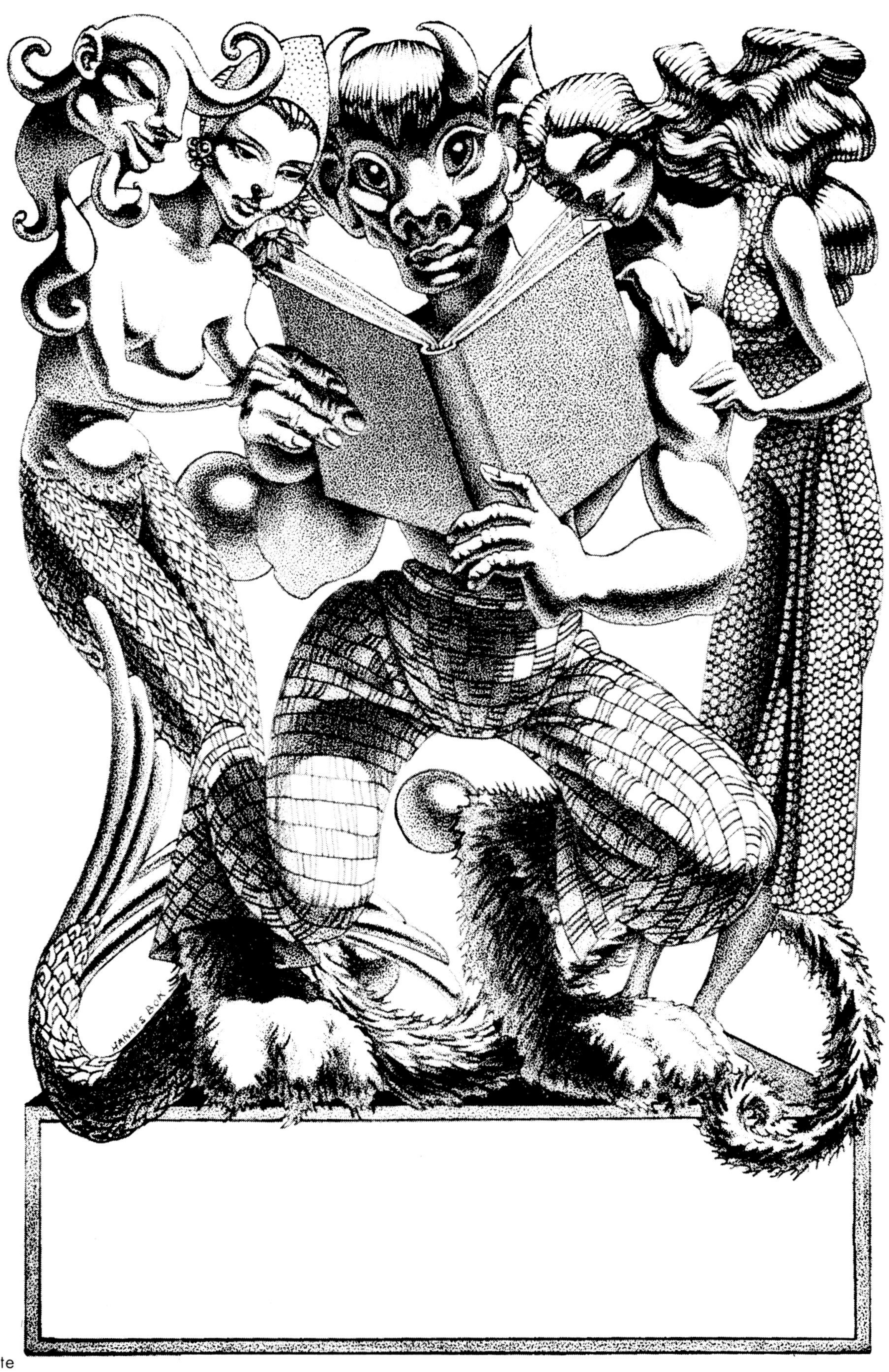

Bookplate

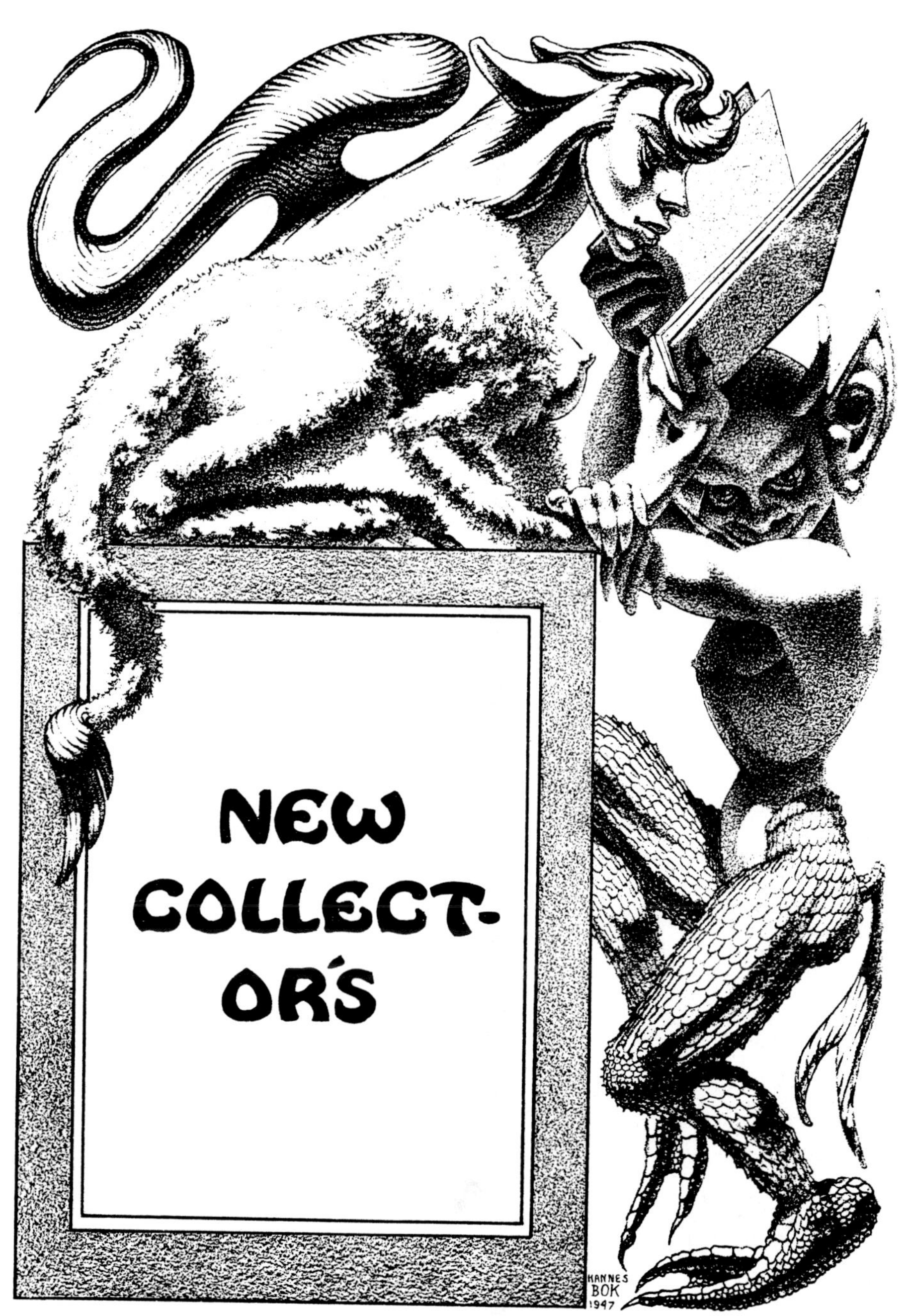

Bookplate

A.MERRITT
The Fox Woman
HANNES BOK
The Blue Pagoda
NEW YORK
BOK

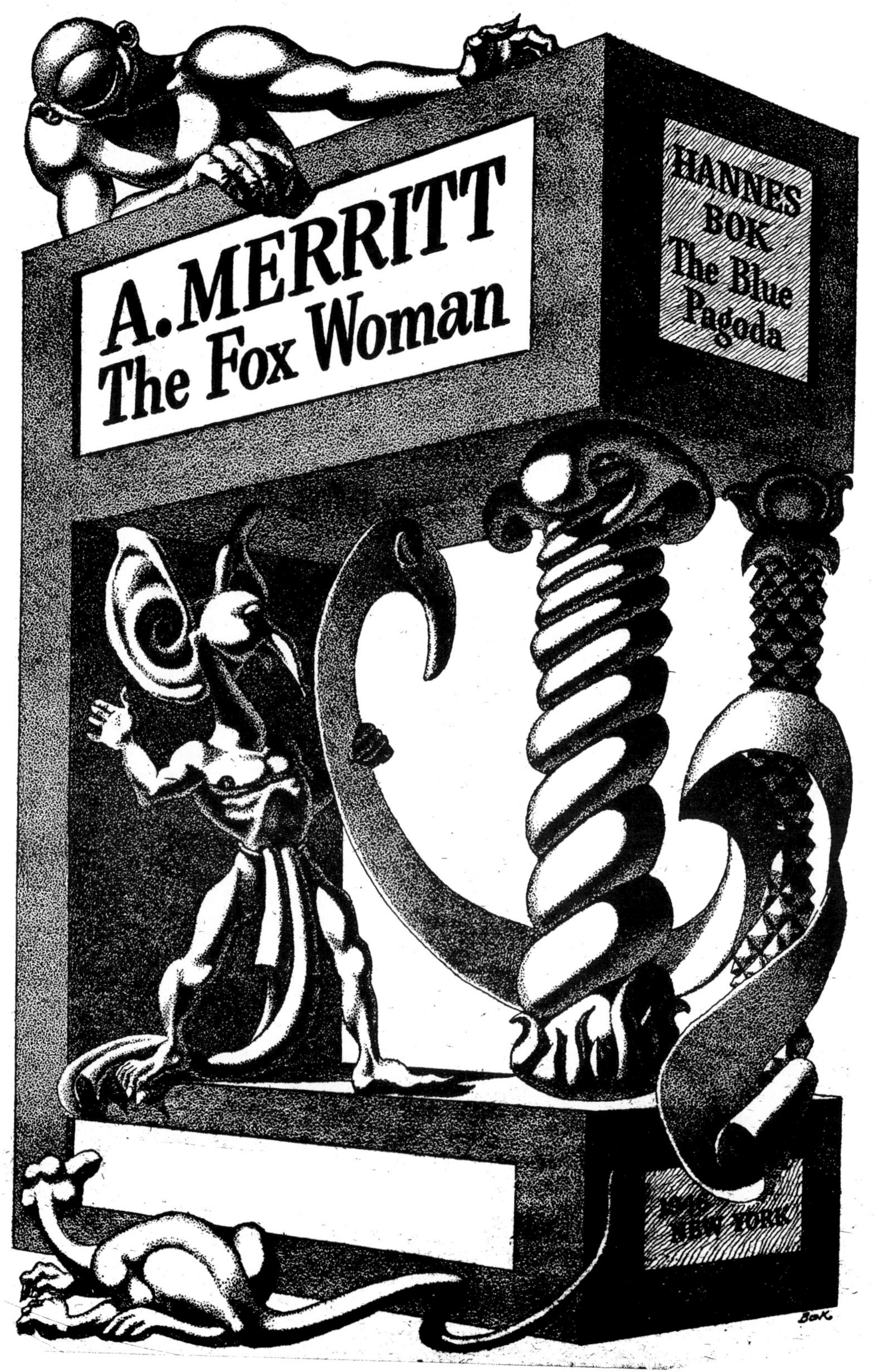

Bookplate

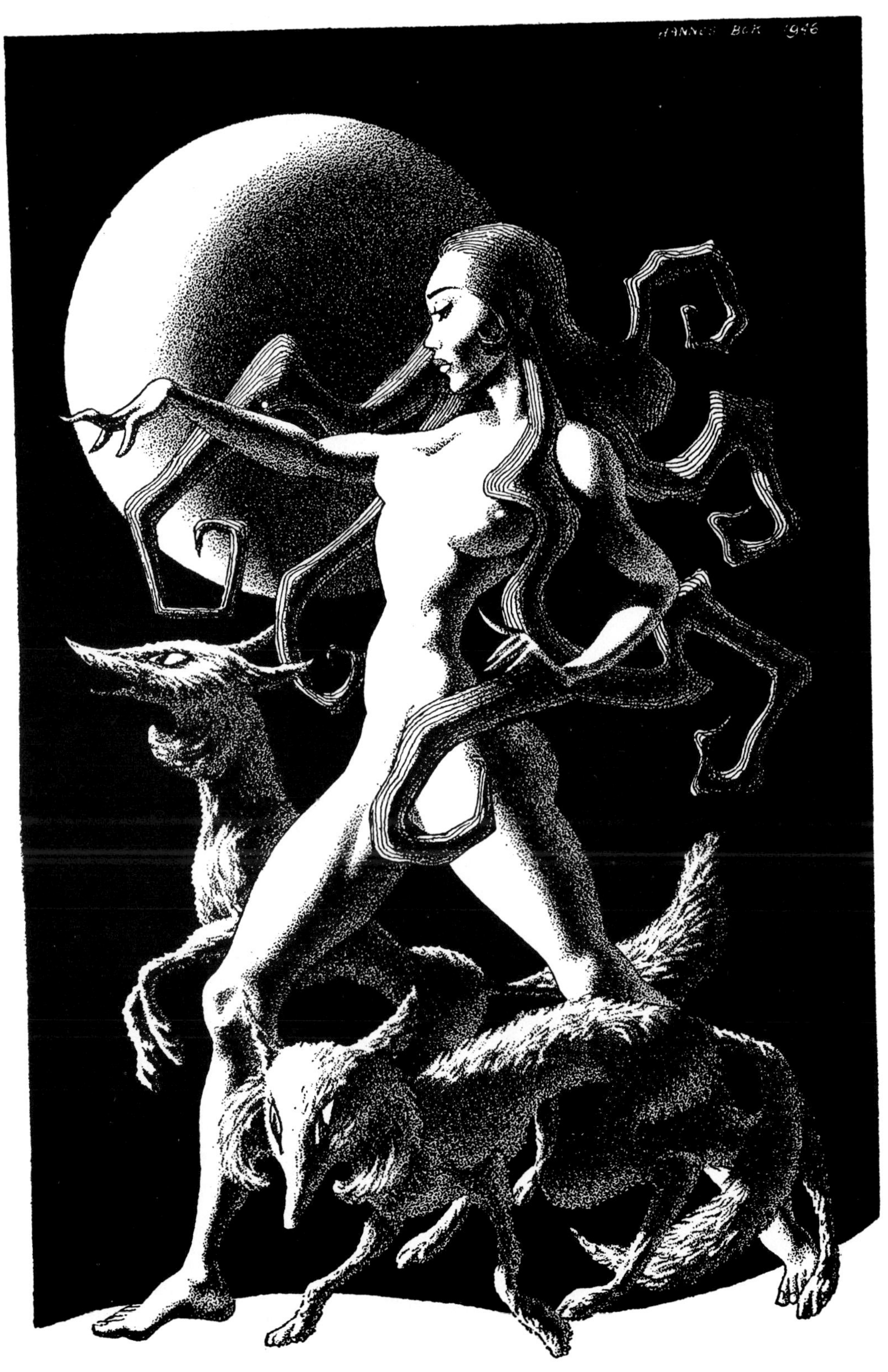

Illustration for "The Fox Woman and the Blue Pagoda" by A. Merritt & Hannes Bok, 1946.

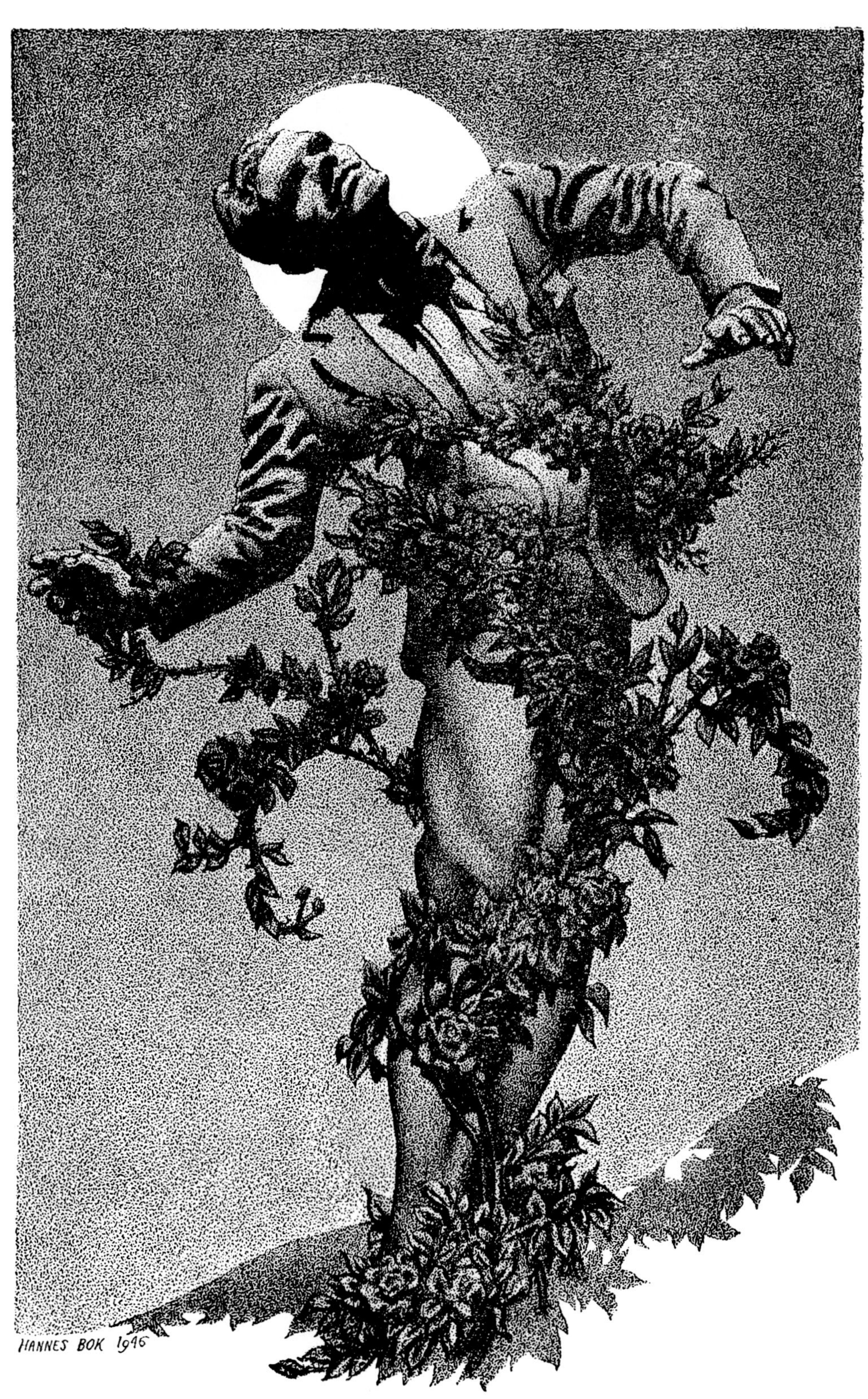

Illustration for "The Fox Woman and the Blue Pagoda" by A. Merritt & Hannes Bok, 1946.

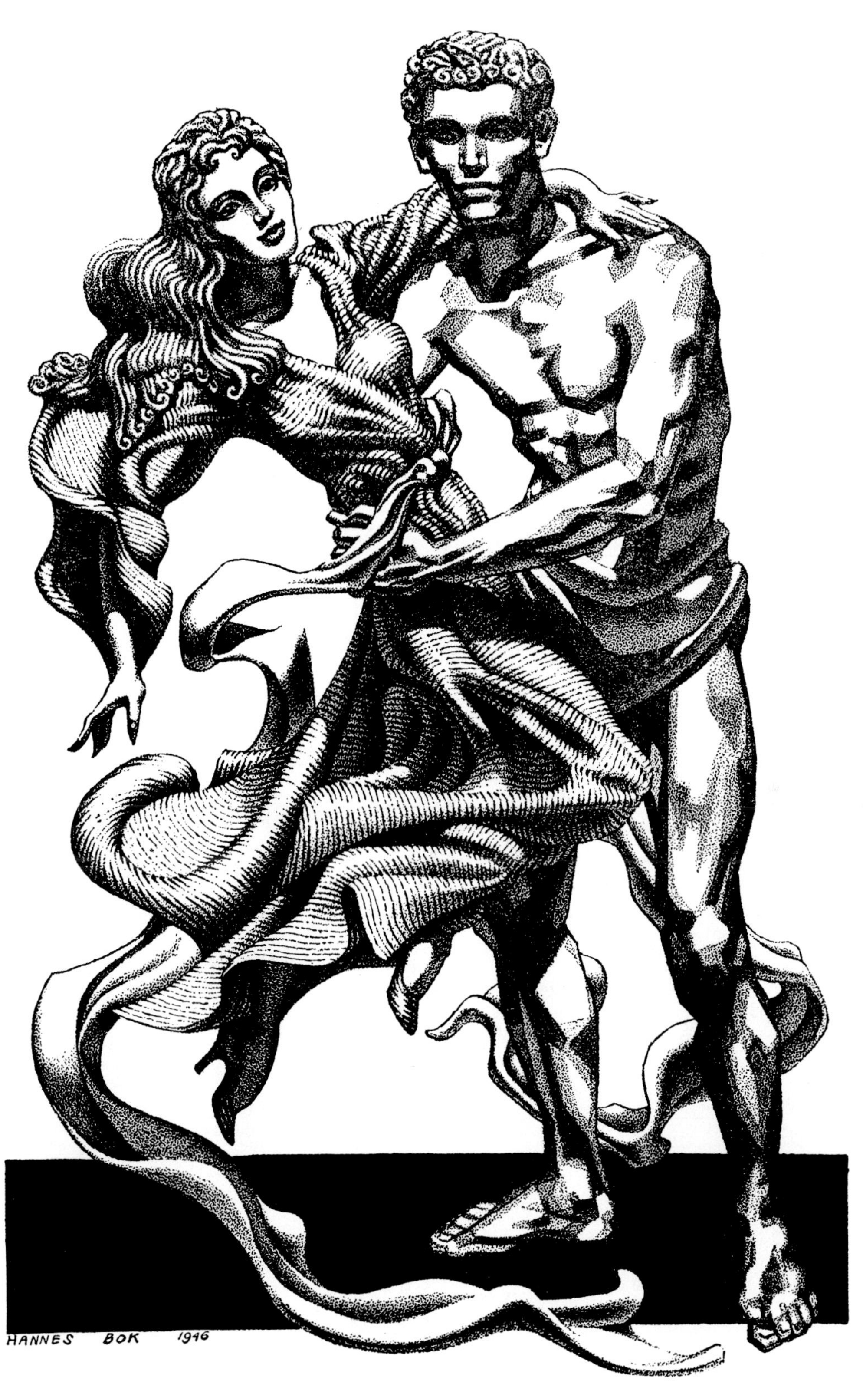

Illustration for "The Fox Woman and the Blue Pagoda" by A. Merritt & Hannes Bok, 1946.

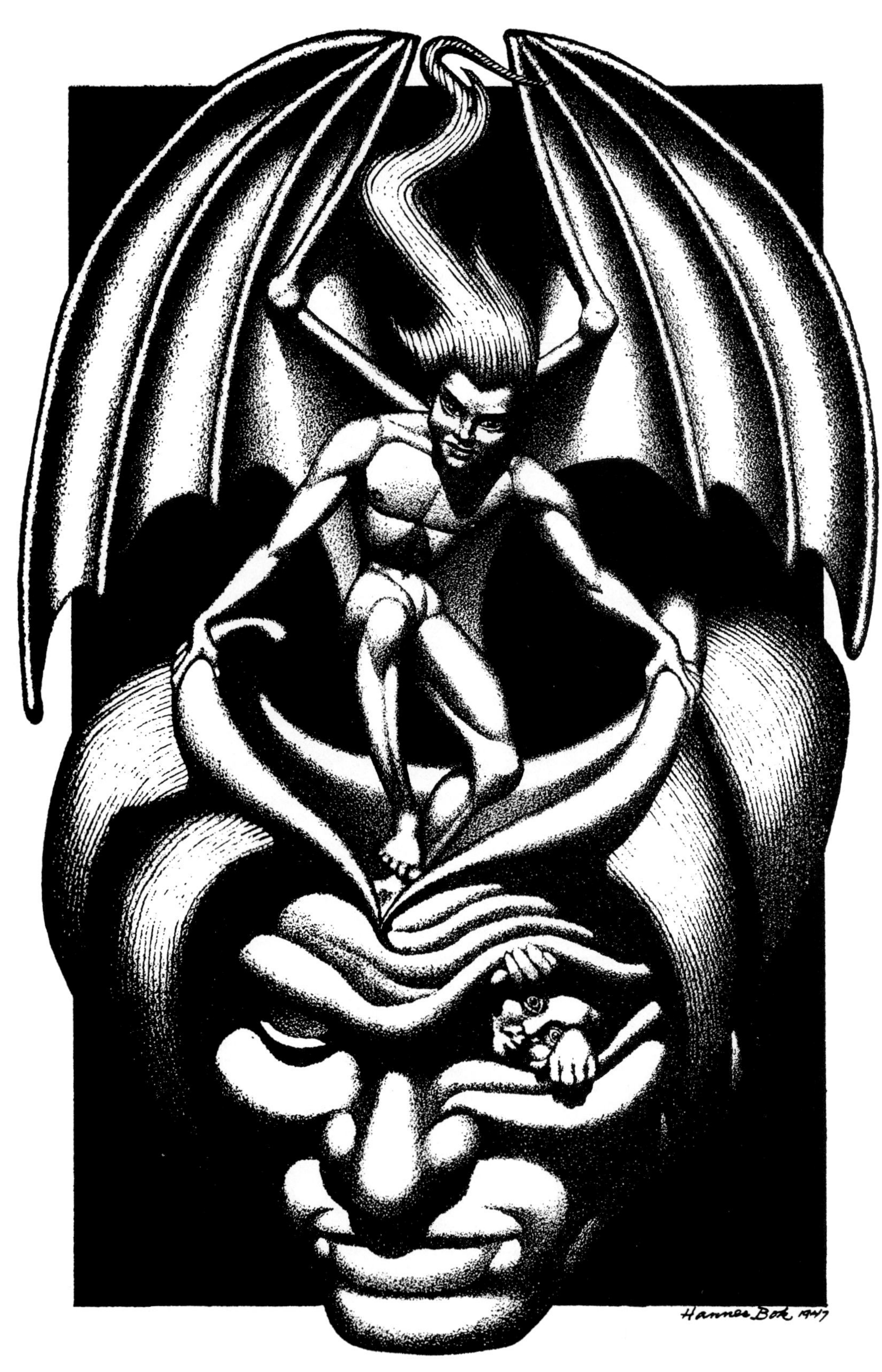

Illustration for "The Black Wheel" by A. Merritt & Hannes Bok, 1947.

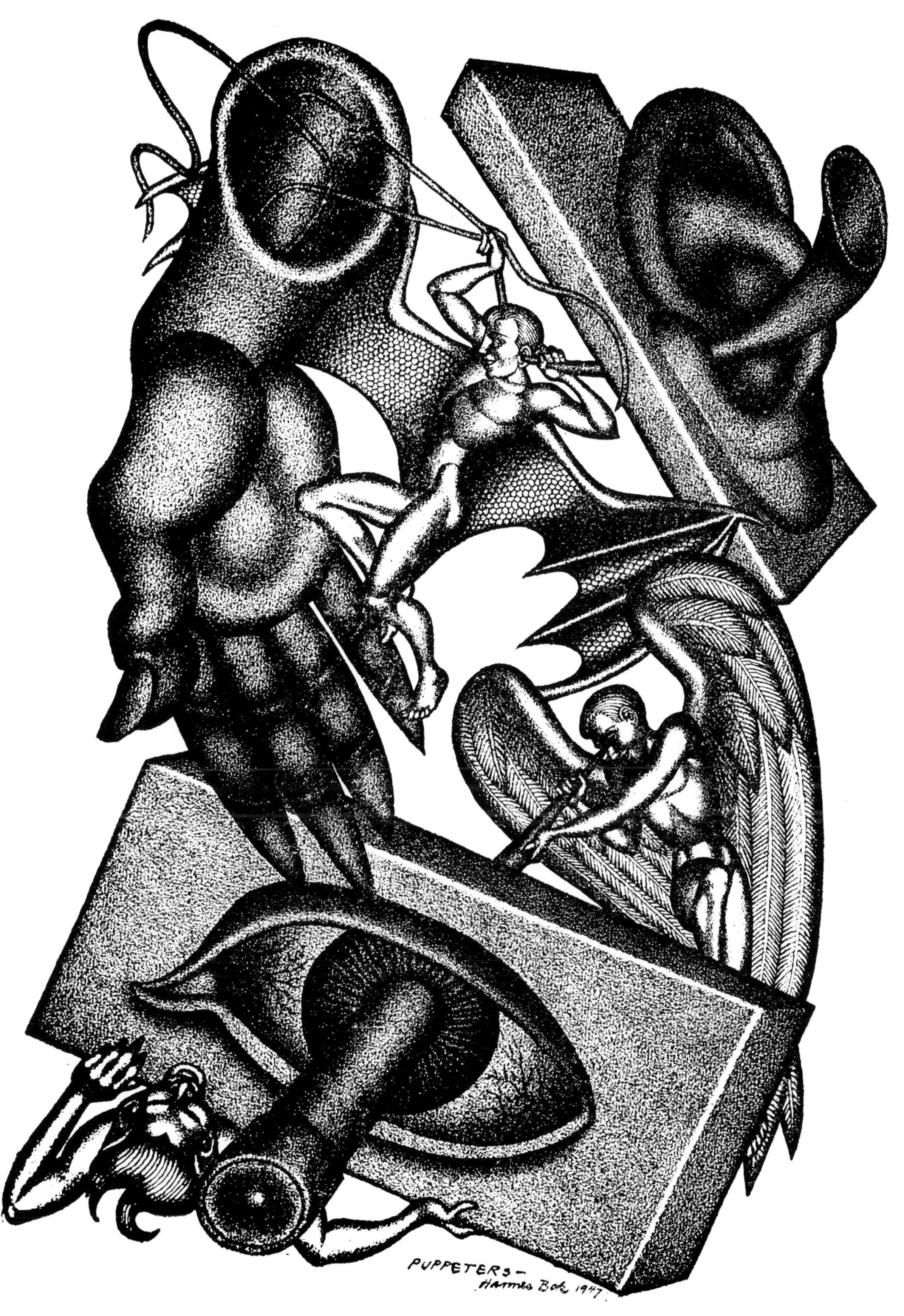

Illustration for "The Black Wheel" by A. Merritt & Hannes Bok, 1947.

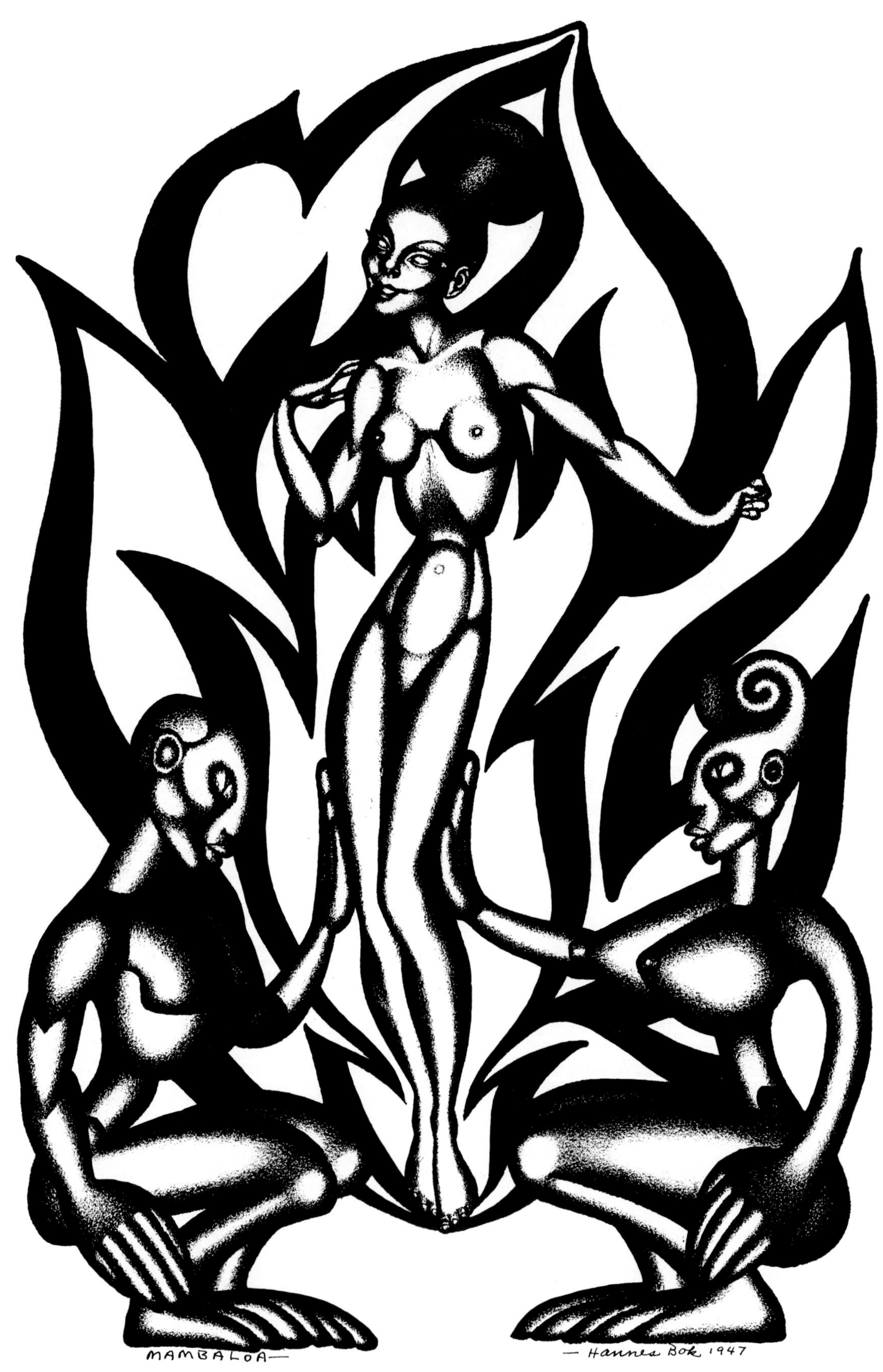

Illustration for "Mambaloa (The Black Wheel)" by A. Merritt & Hannes Bok, 1947.

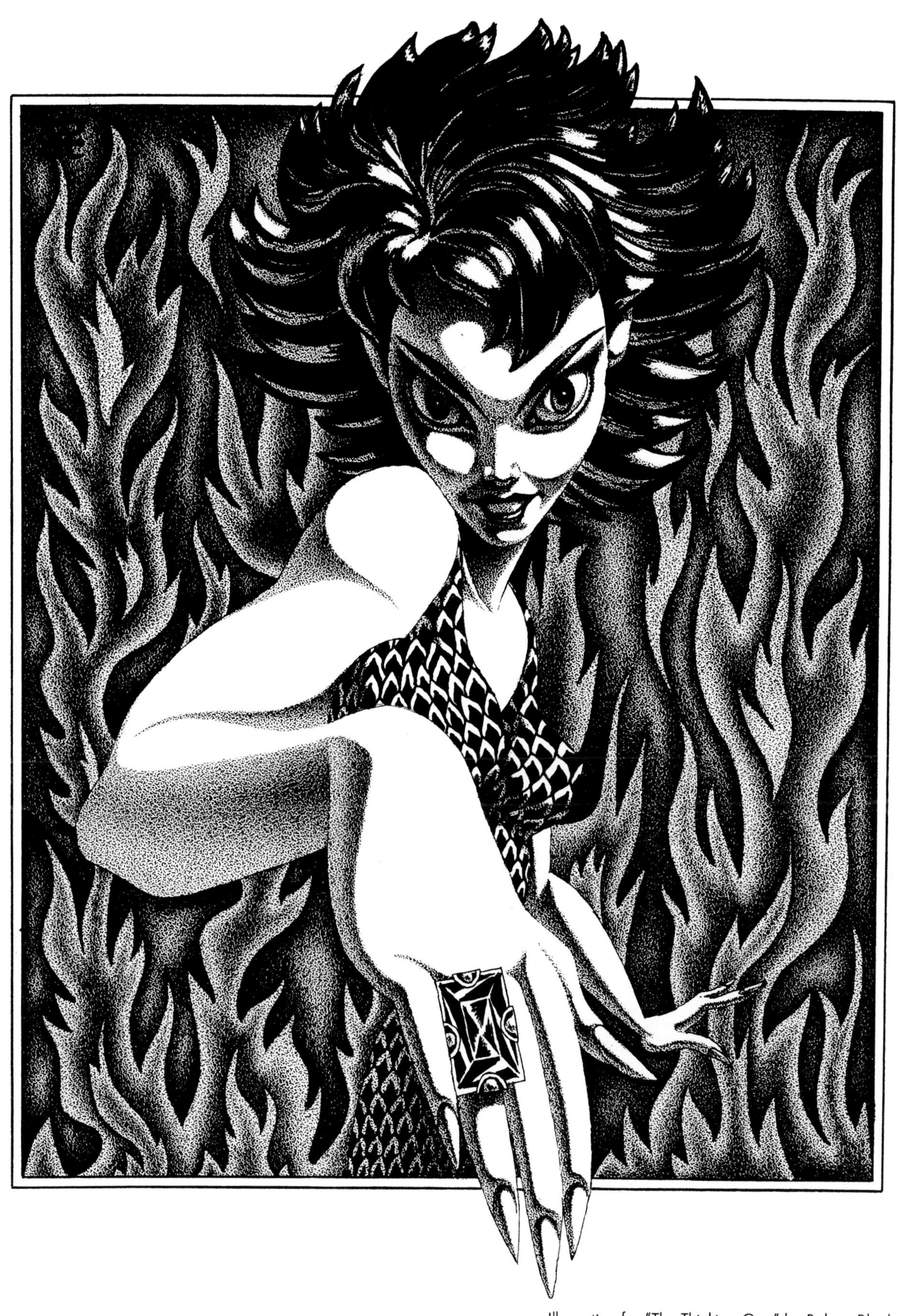

Illustration for "The Thinking Cap" by Robert Bloch, 1953.

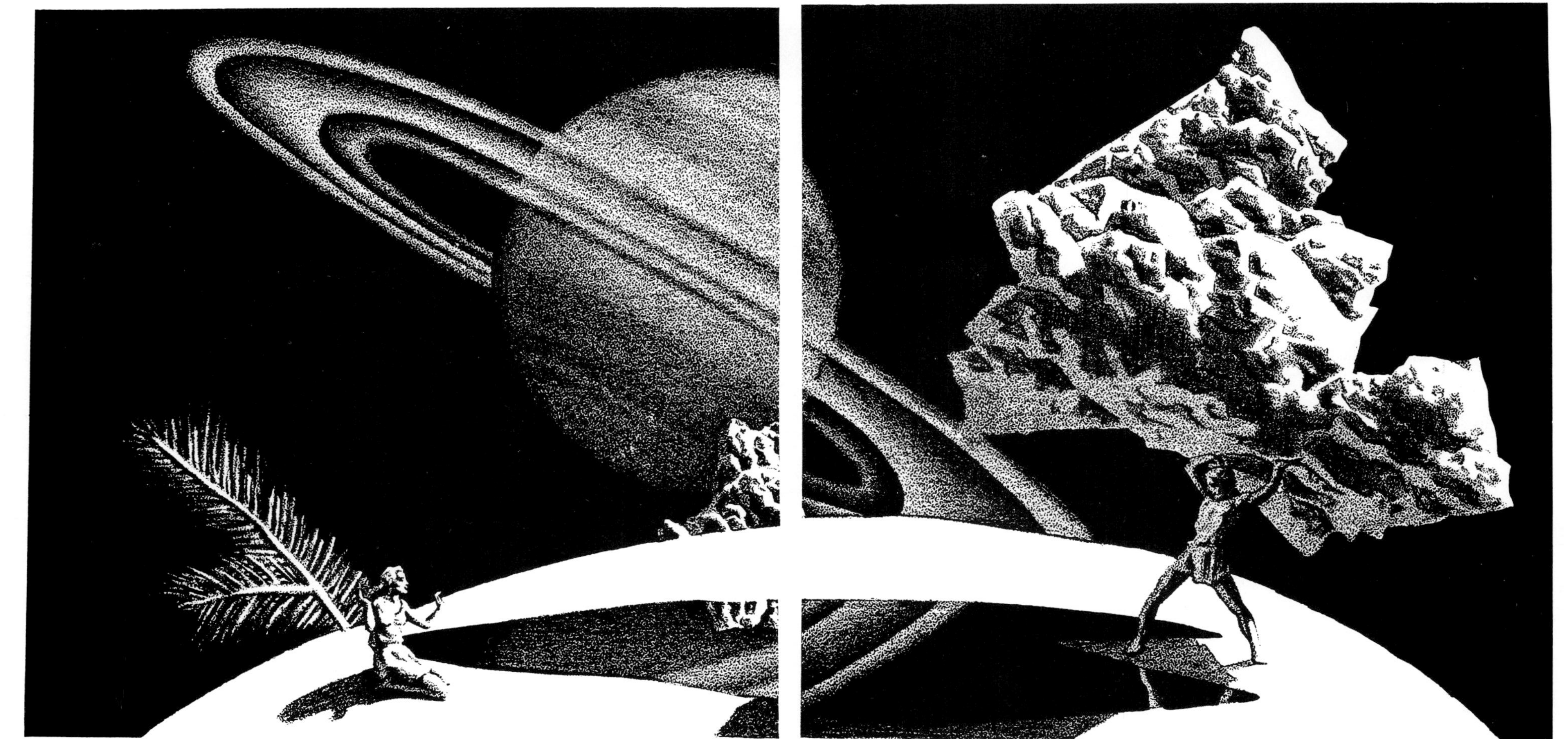

Black and white illustration

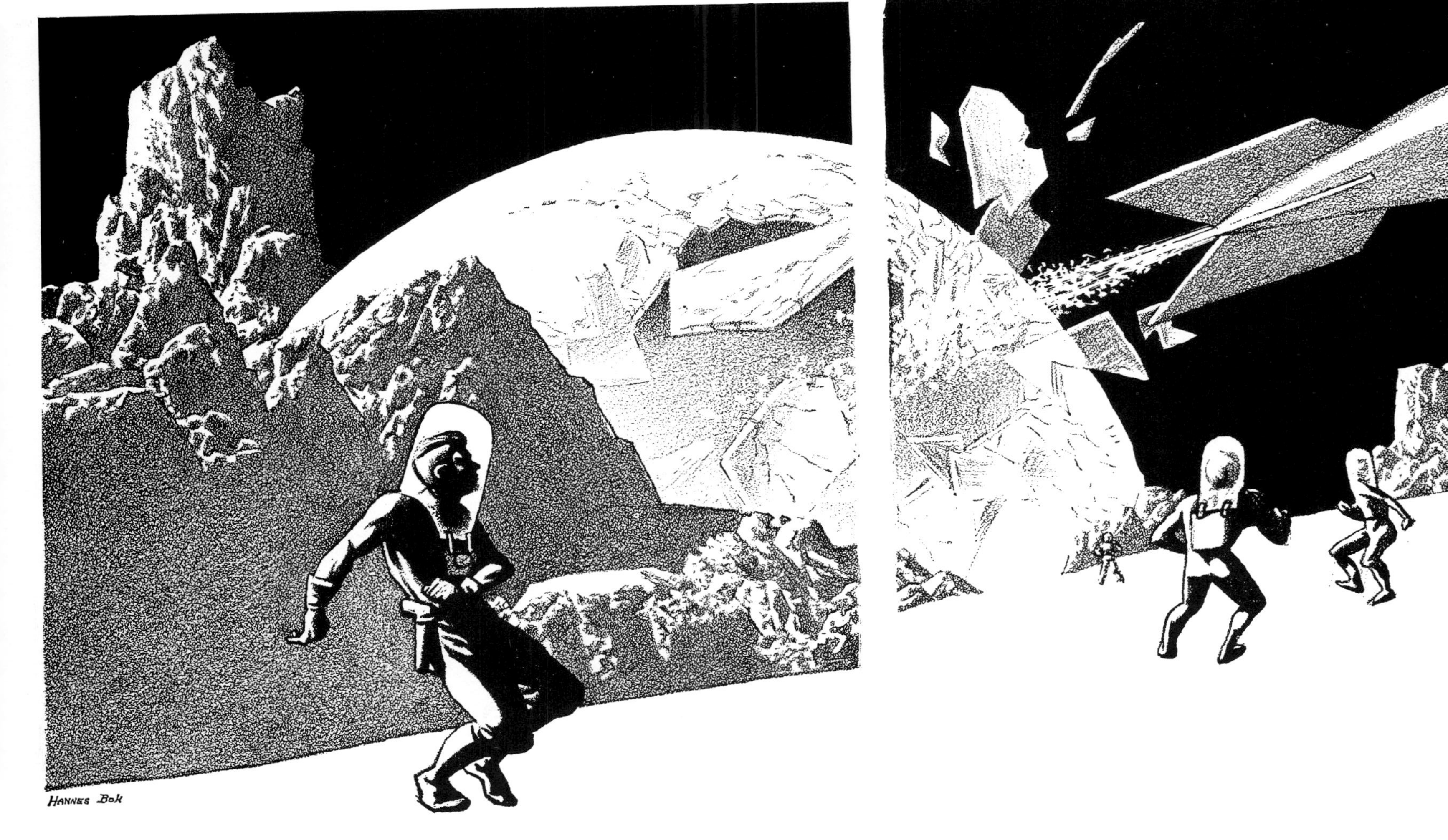

Black and white illustration

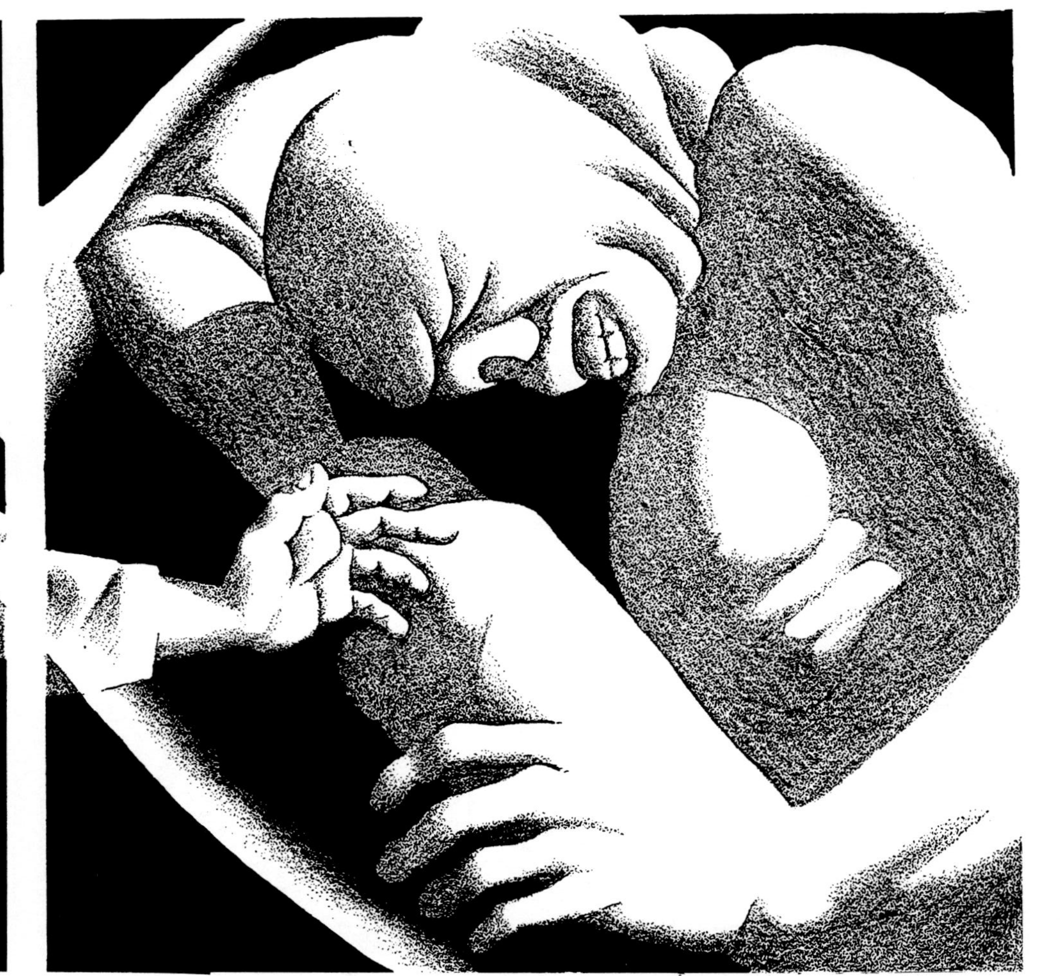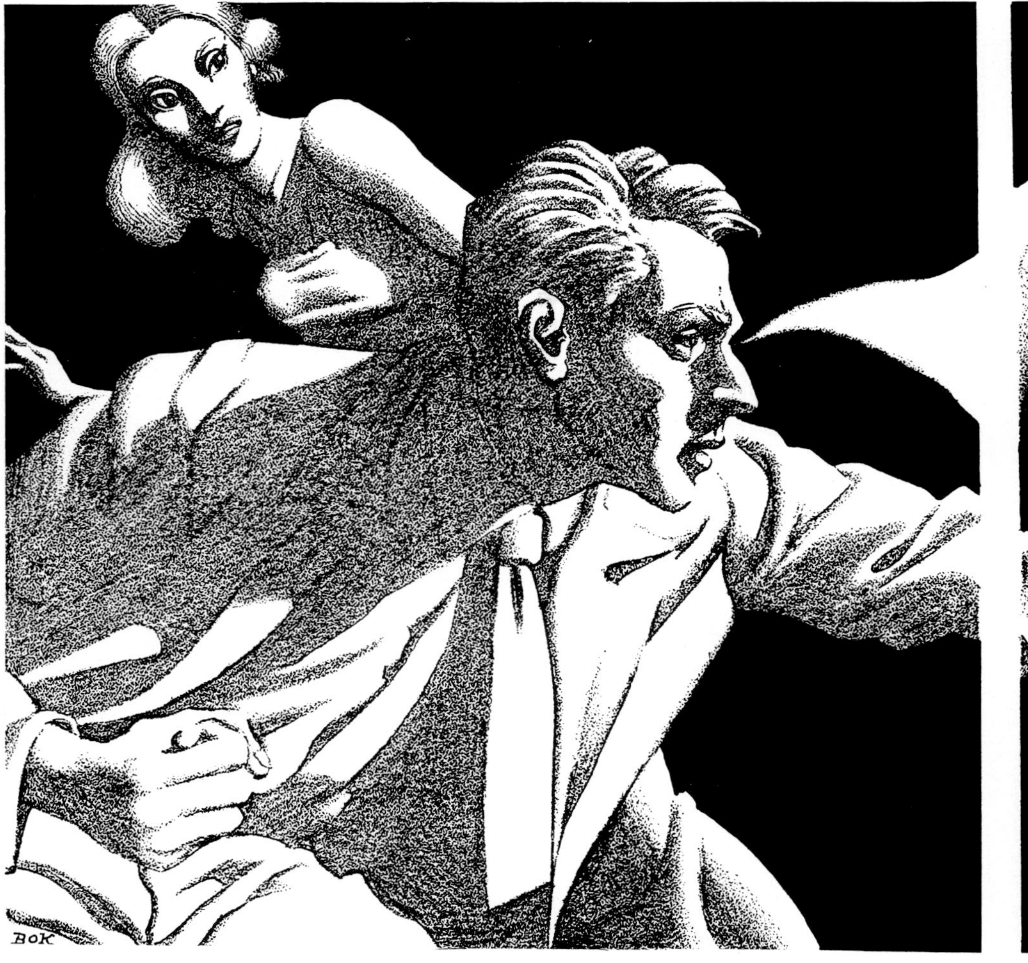

Black and white illustration

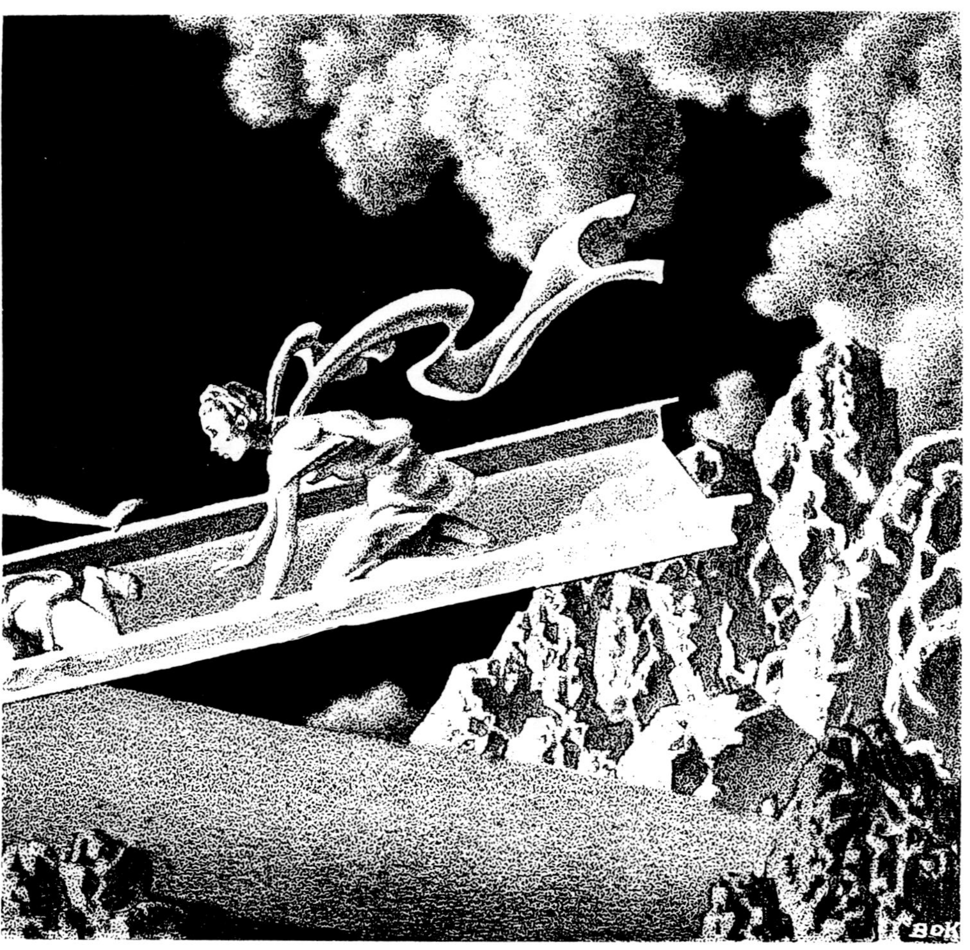

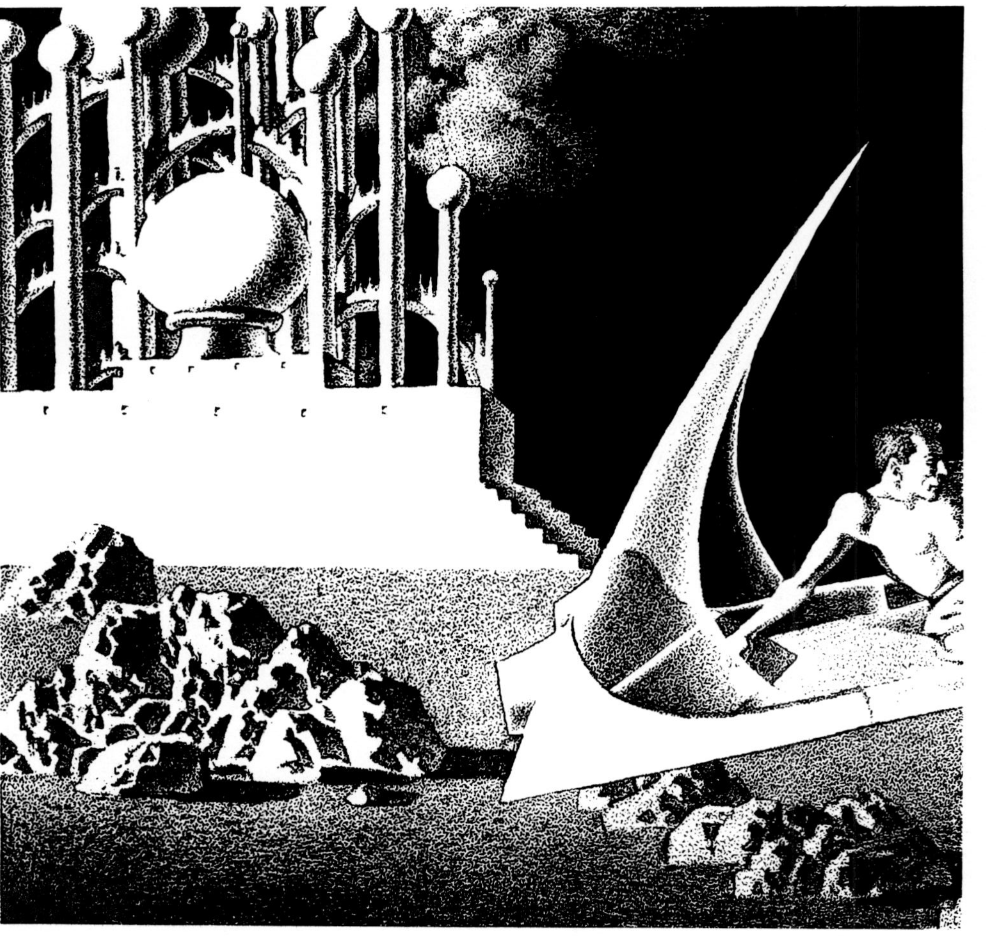

Black and white illustration

69

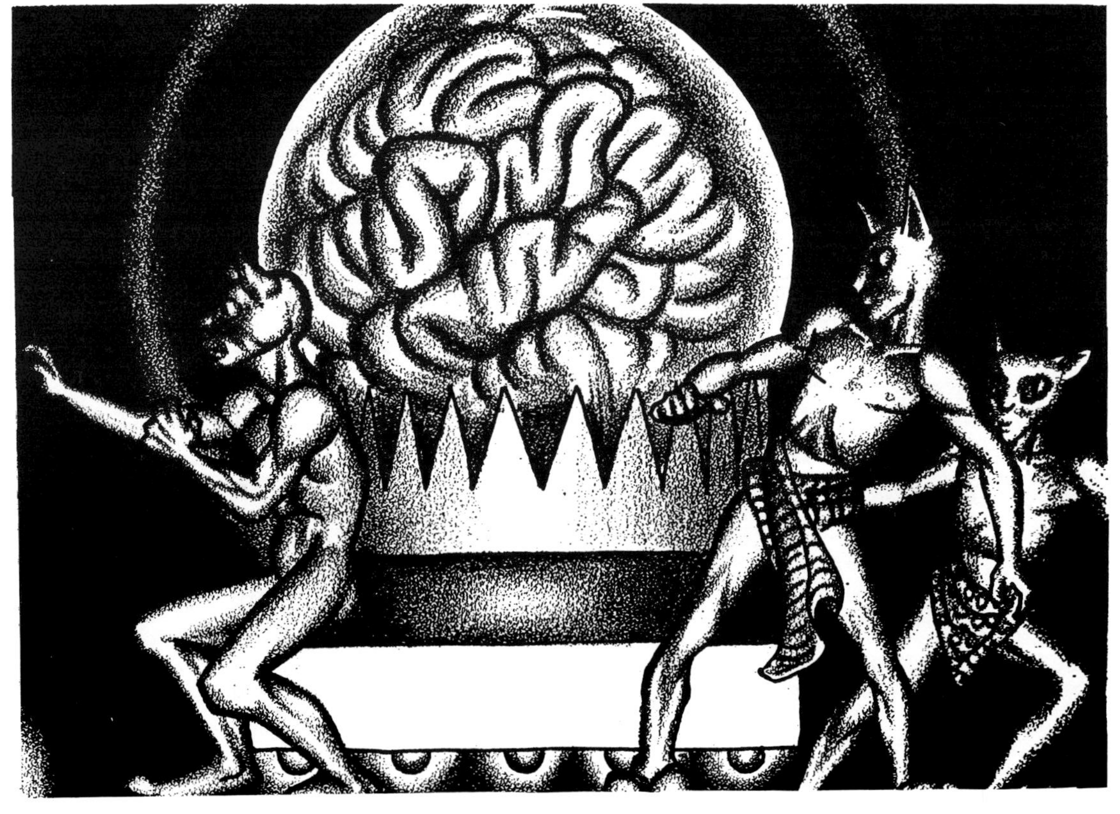

Black and white illustration

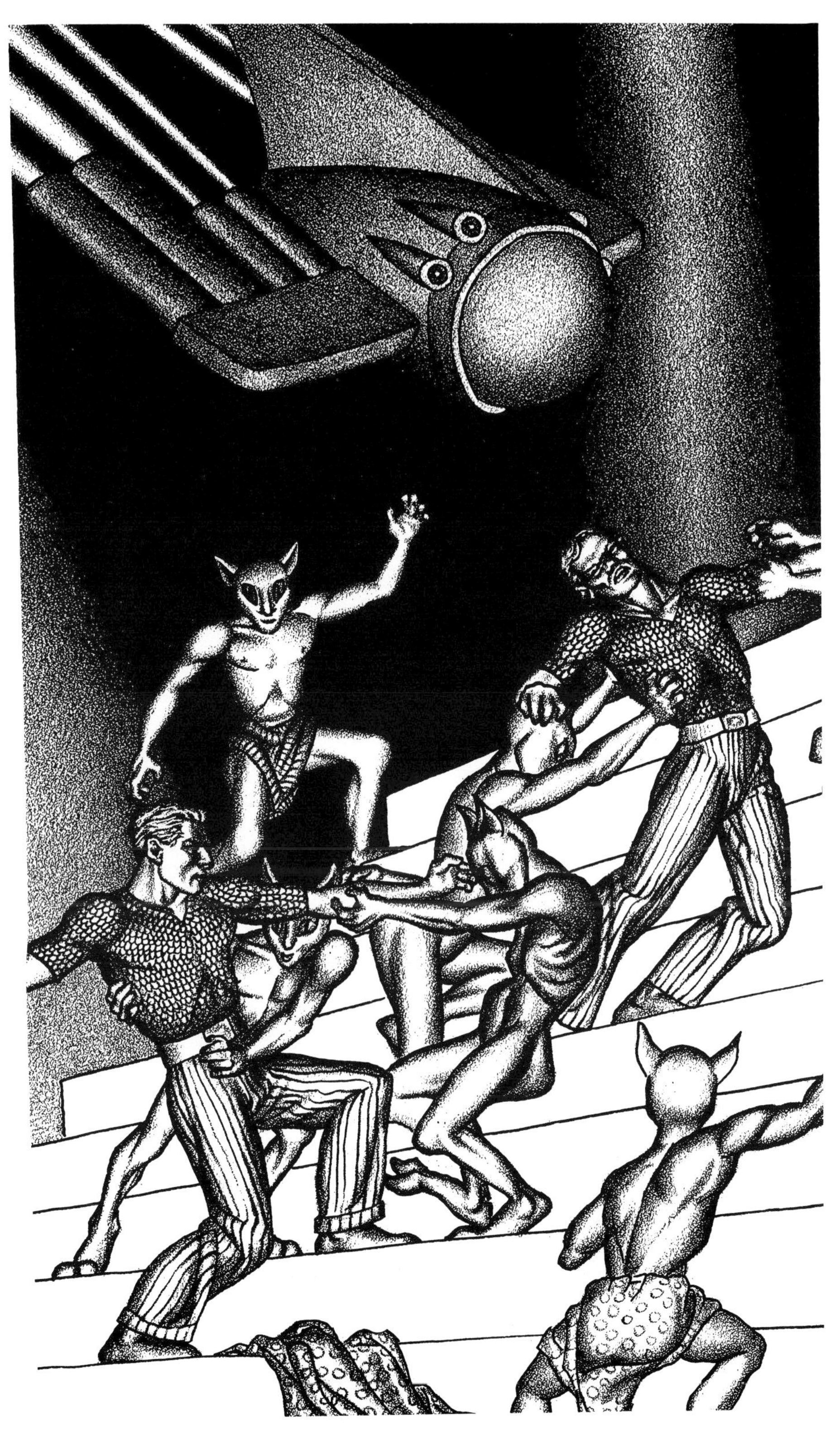

Black and white illustration

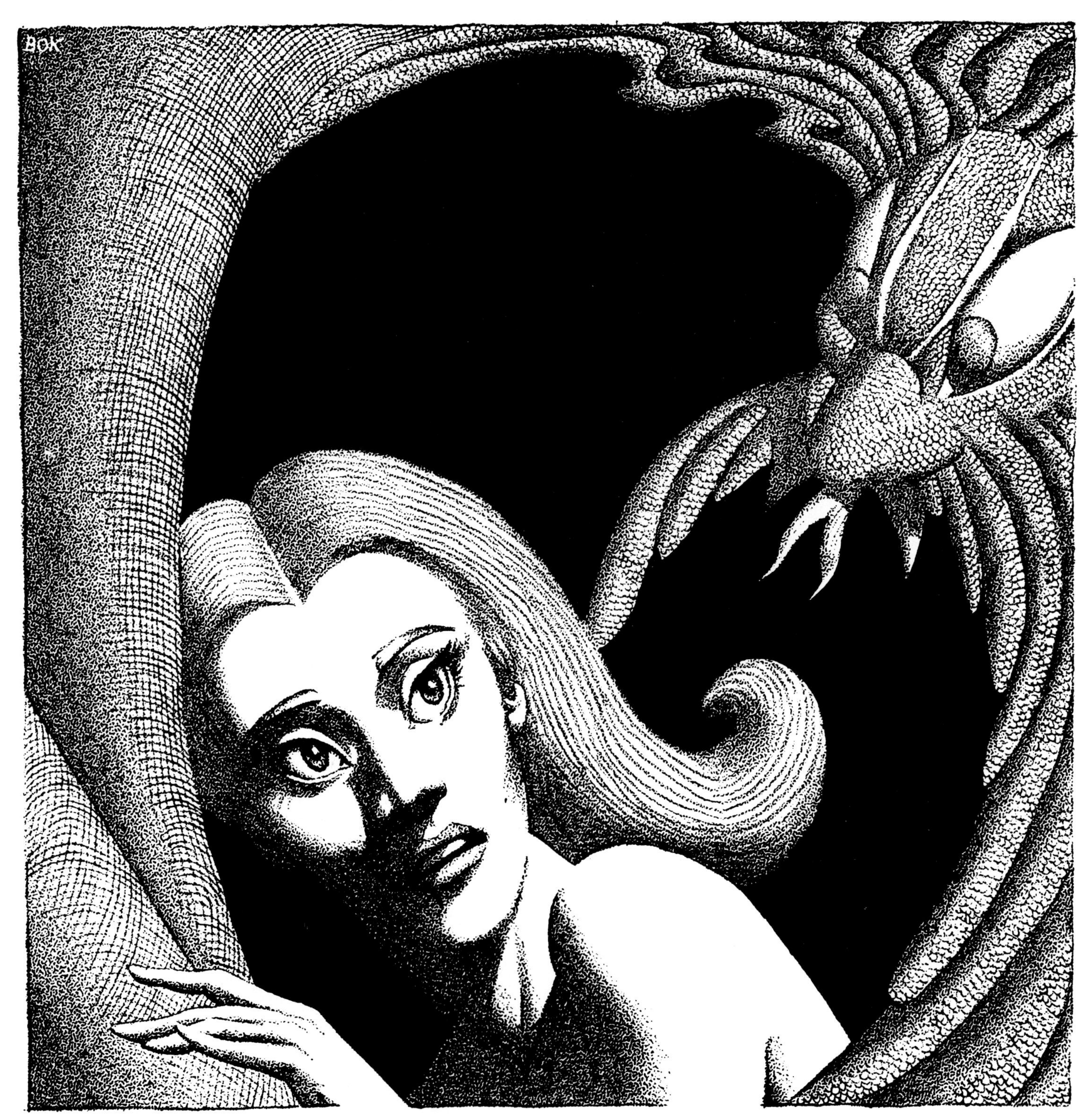

Illustration for "Lost Legion" by Lyle Monroe (Pseudonym of Robert A. Heinlein), 1941.

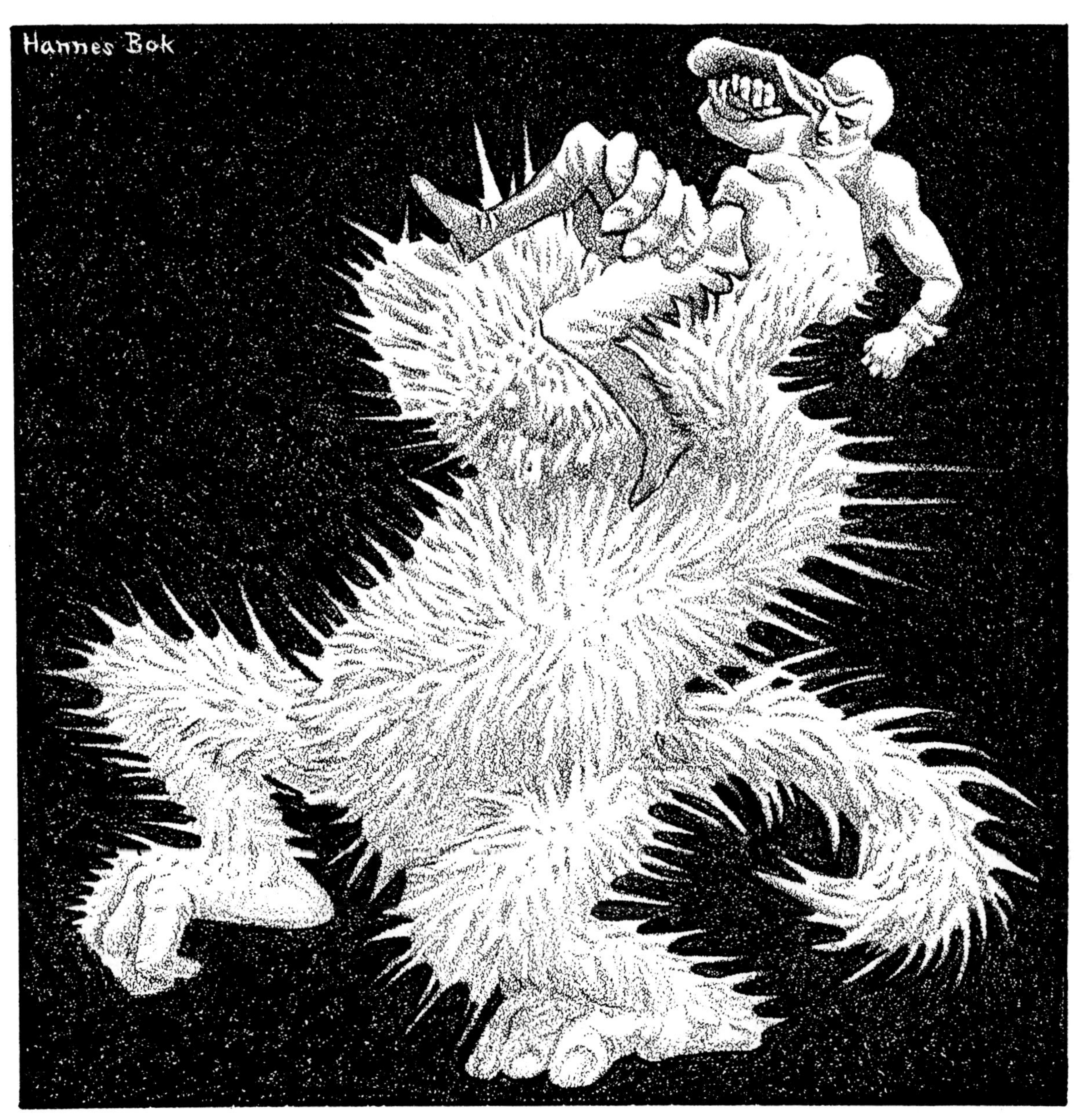

Illustration for "Stepson of Mars" by Ivar Towers, 1940.

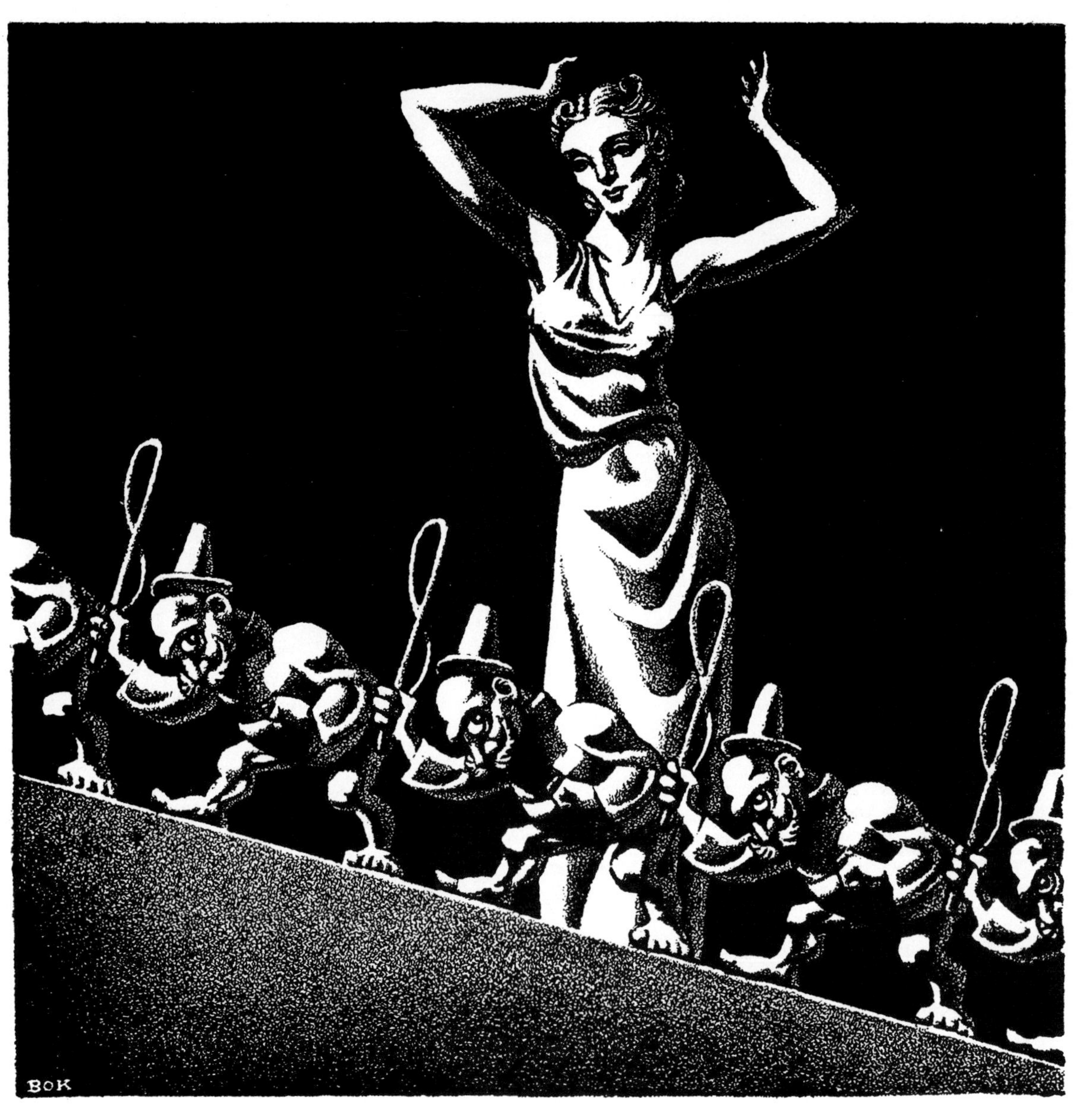

Illustration for "The Improbable" by Charles R. Tanner, 1941.

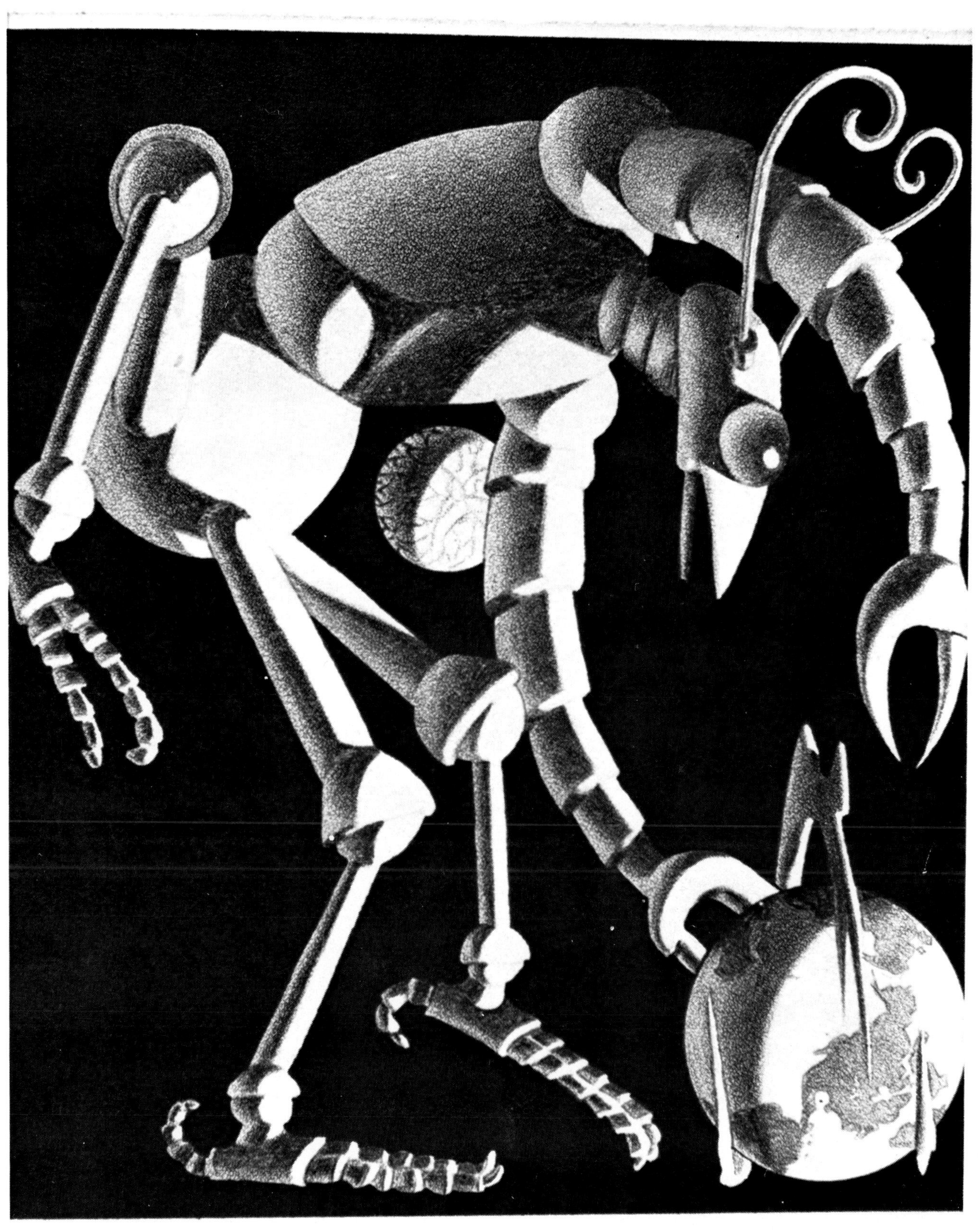

Black and white illustration

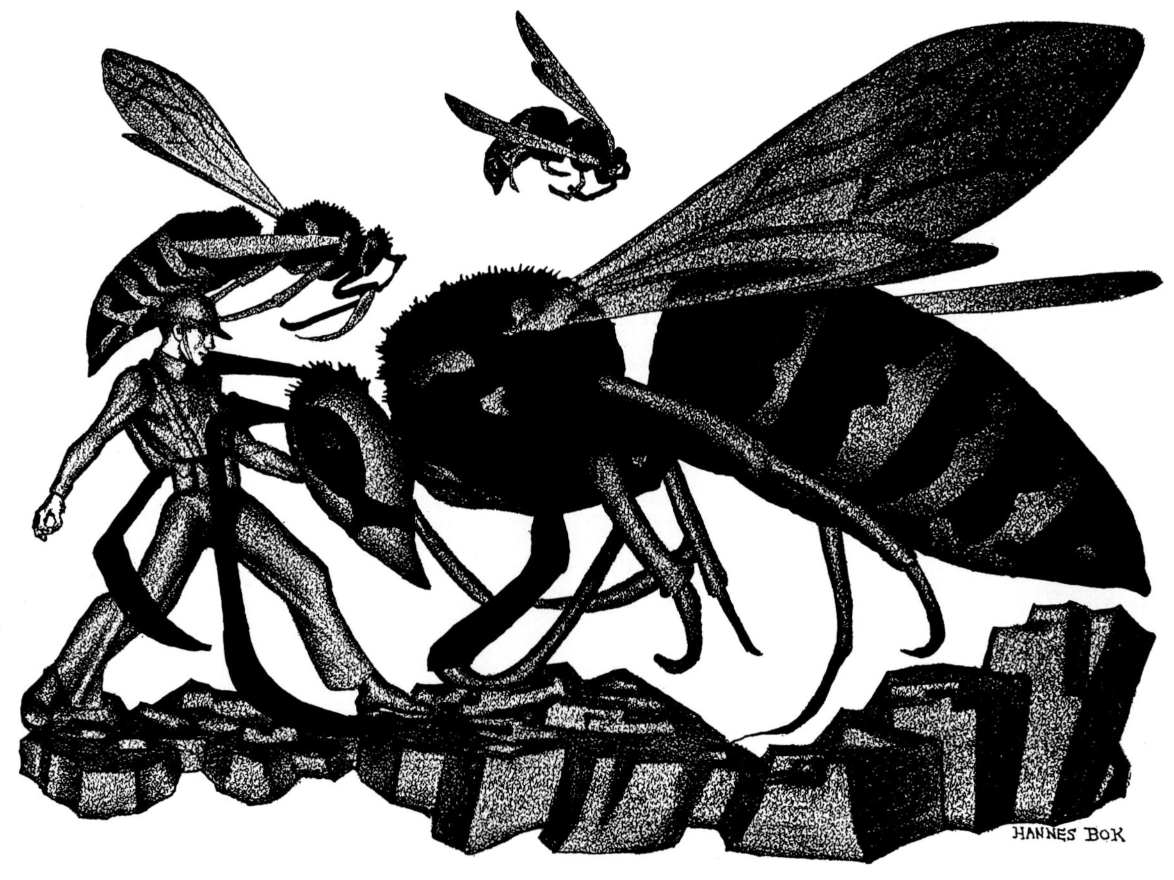

Illustration for "The Sky Terror" by Ed Earl Repp, 1941.

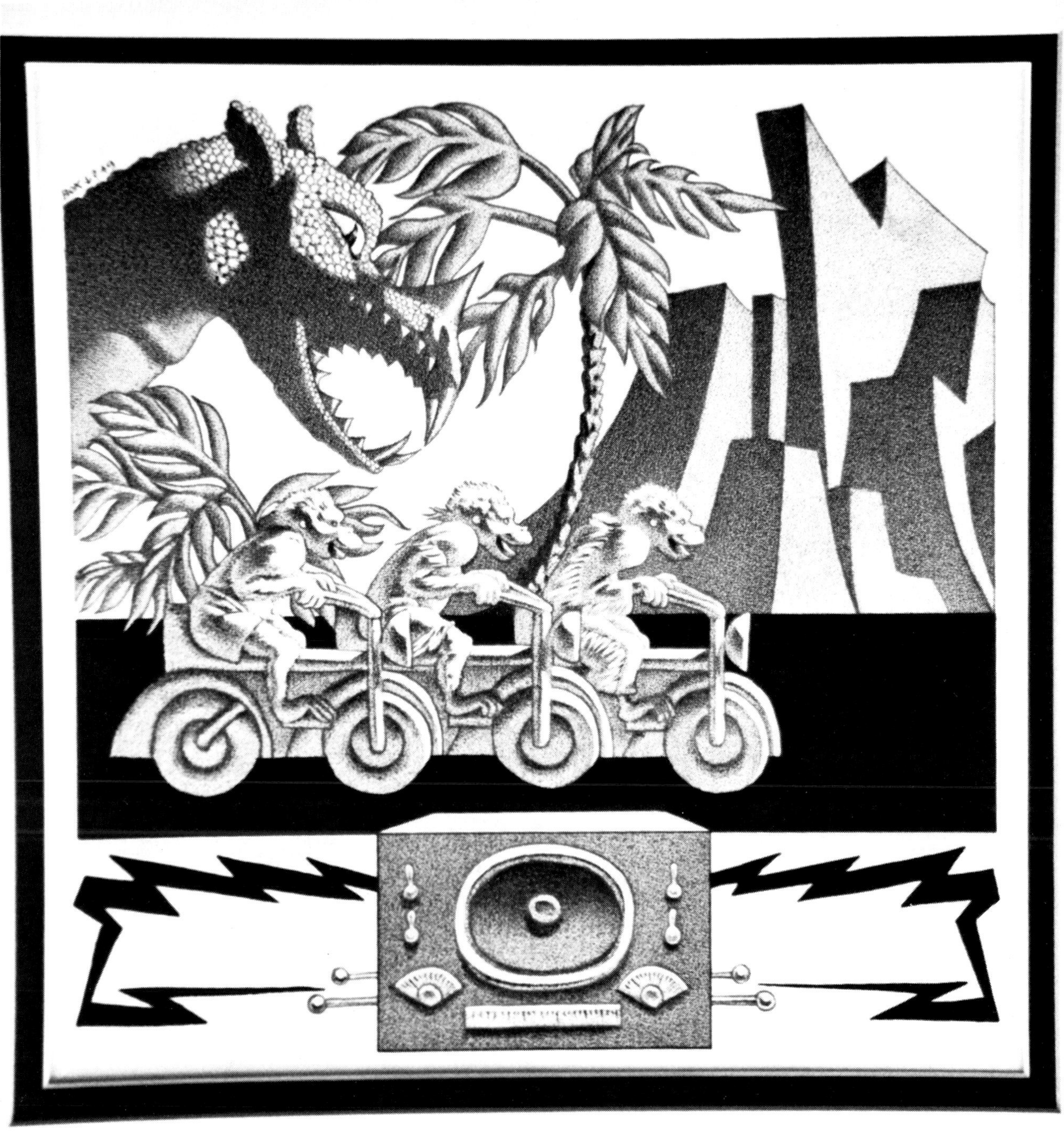

Black and white illustration

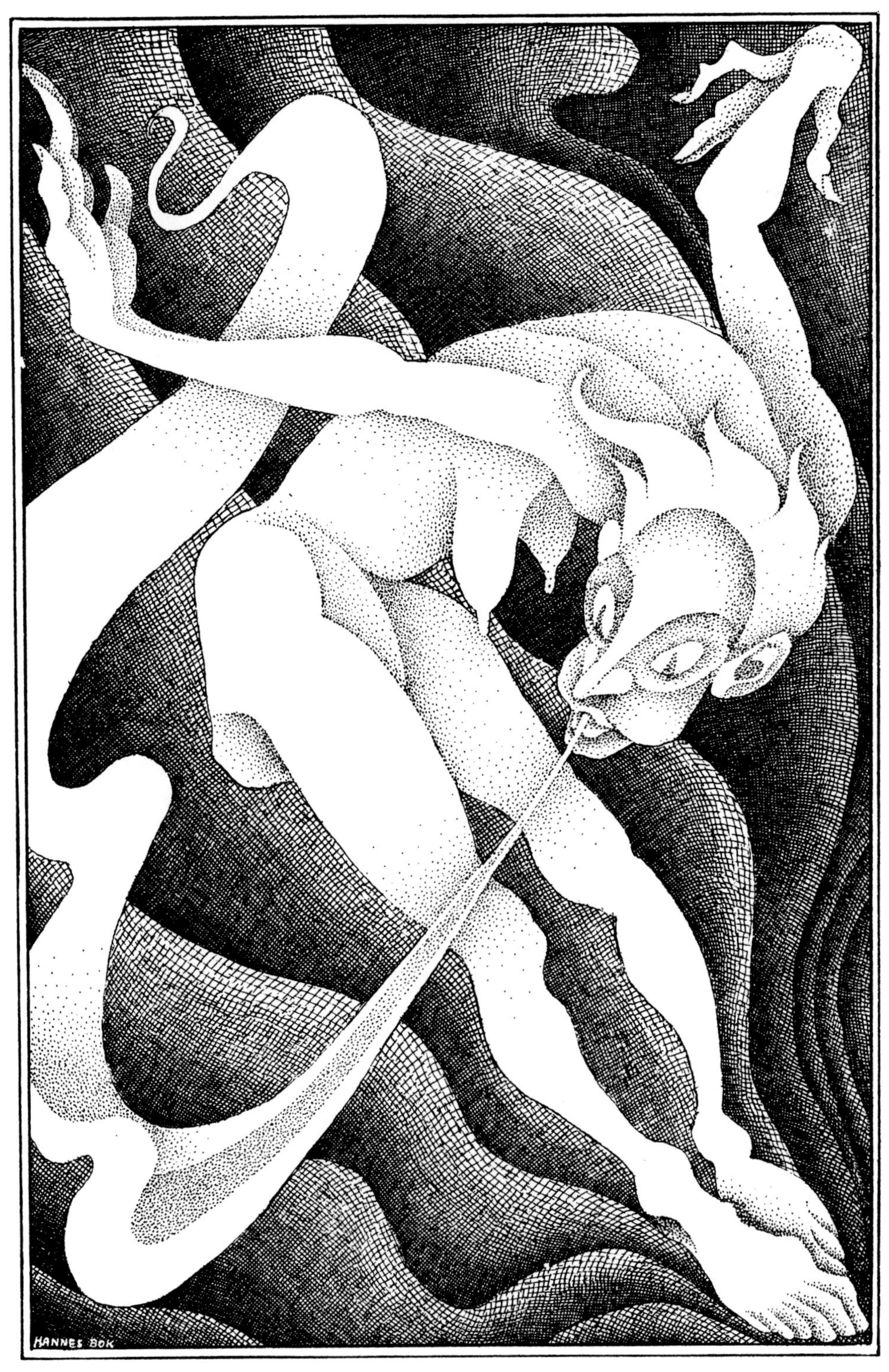

Illustration for "The Wind," 1941.

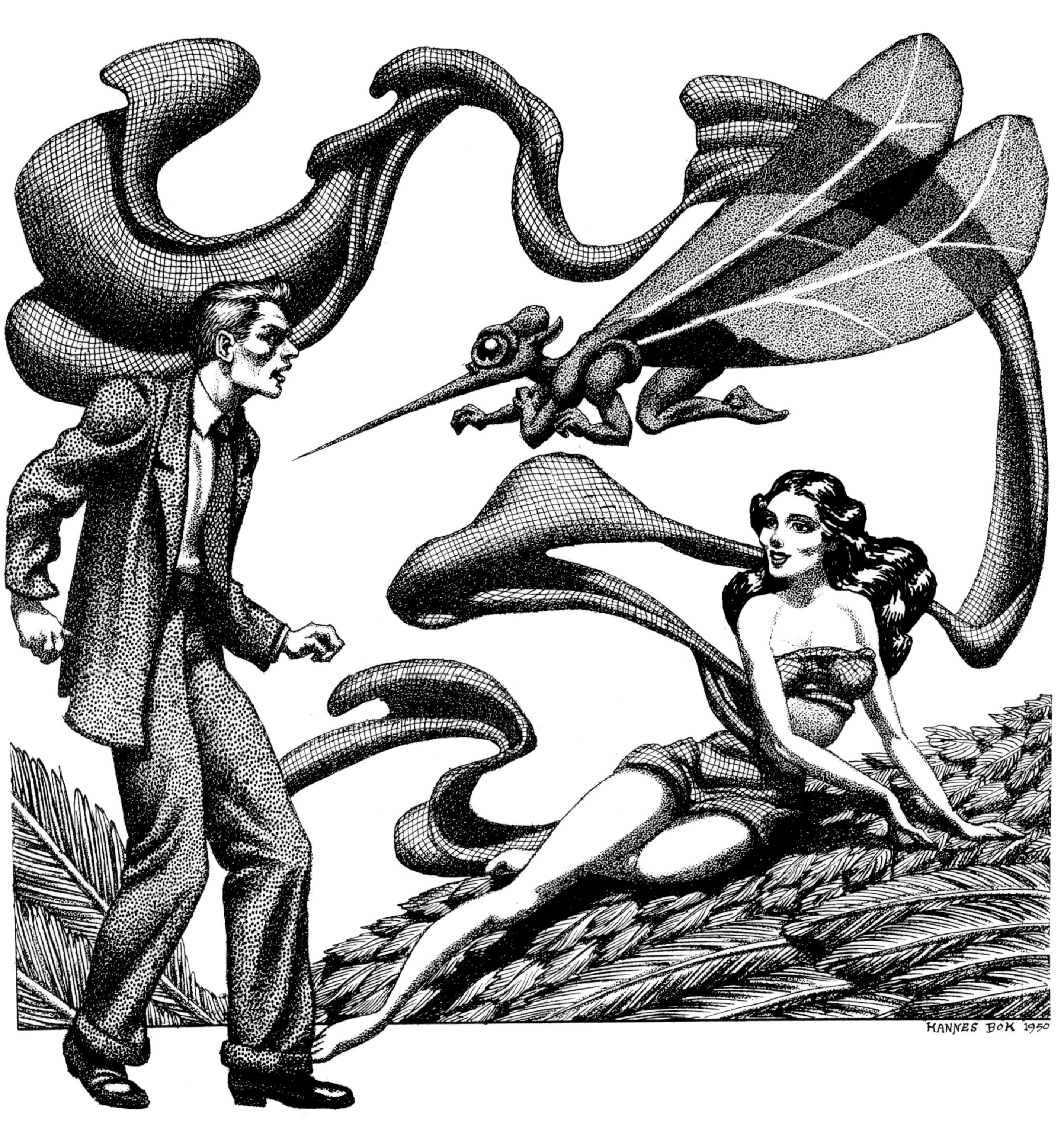

Illustration for "Soul Stealers" by Chester S. Geier, 1950.

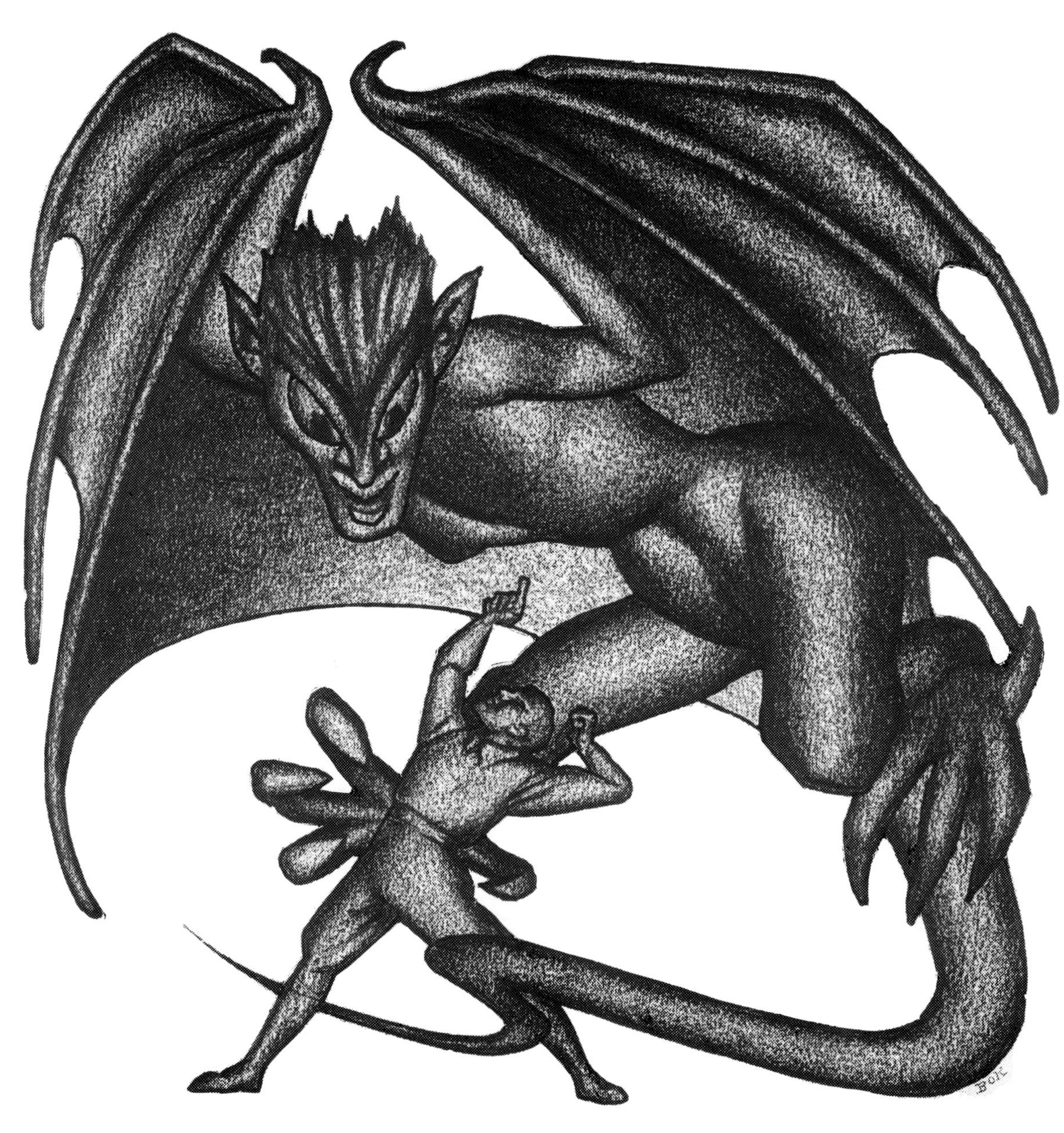

Illustration for "Pit of Doom" by David H. Keller, 1942.

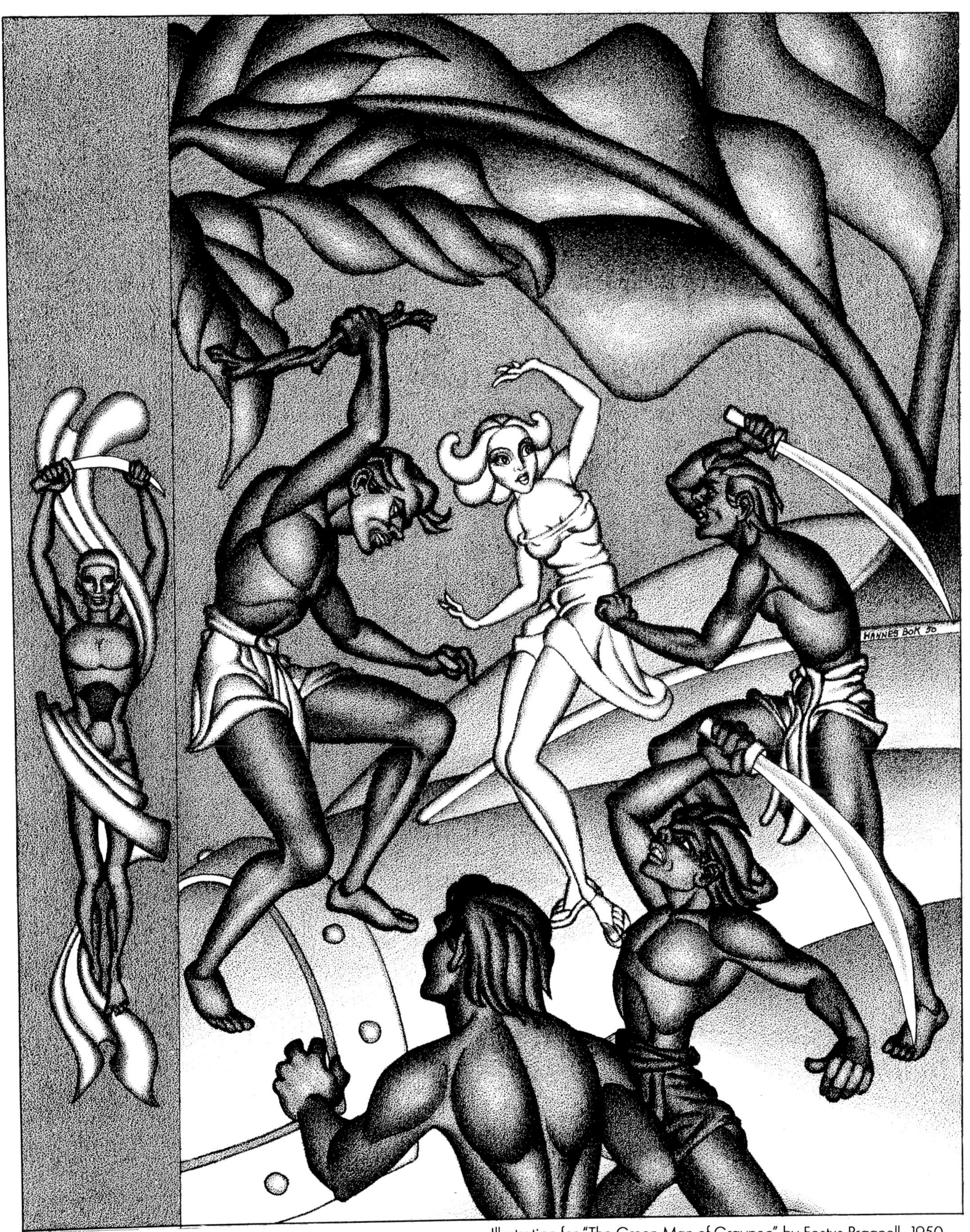

Illustration for "The Green Man of Graypec" by Festus Pragnell, 1950.

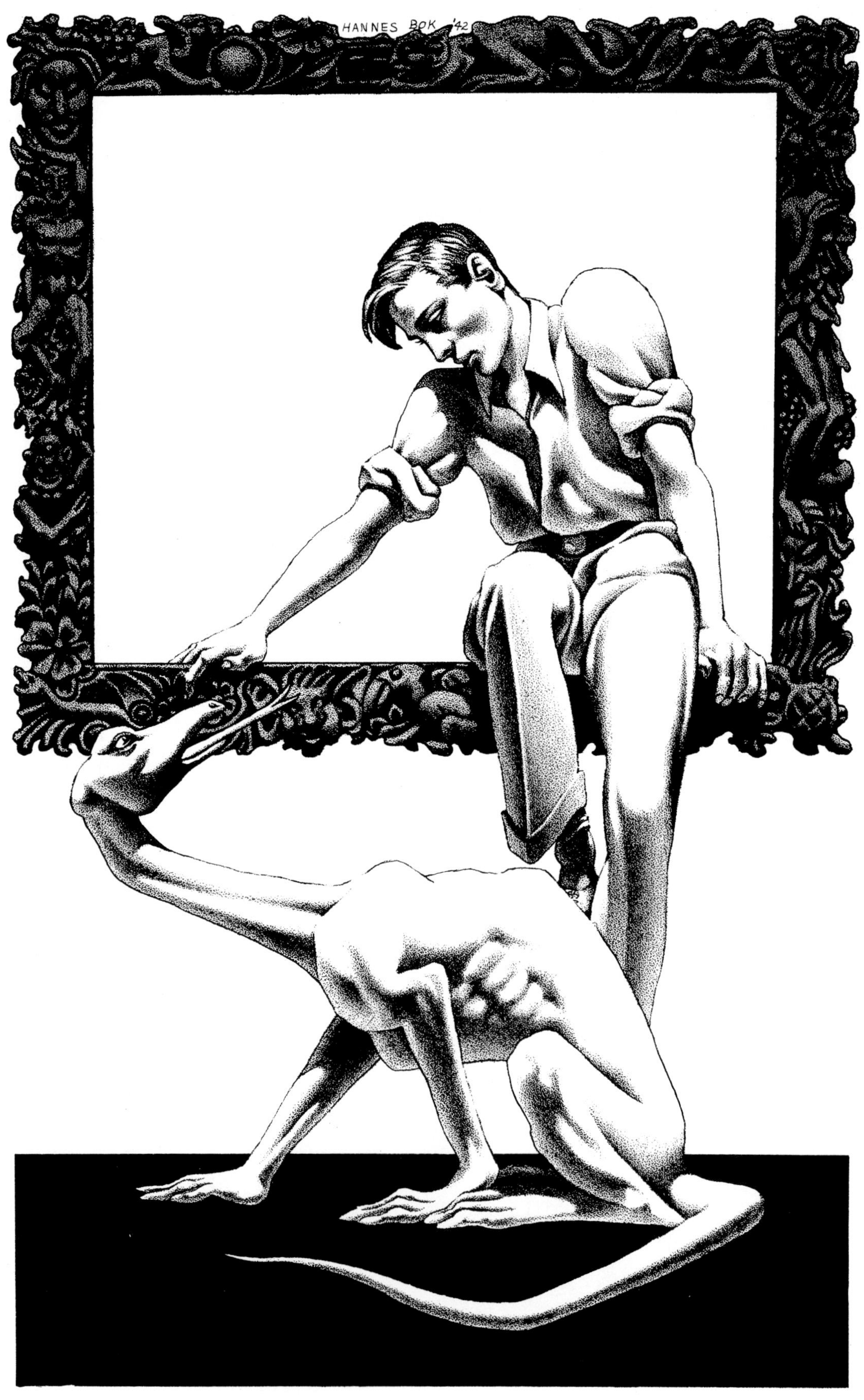

Illustration for "Dimensional Doors" by Hannes Bok, 1944.

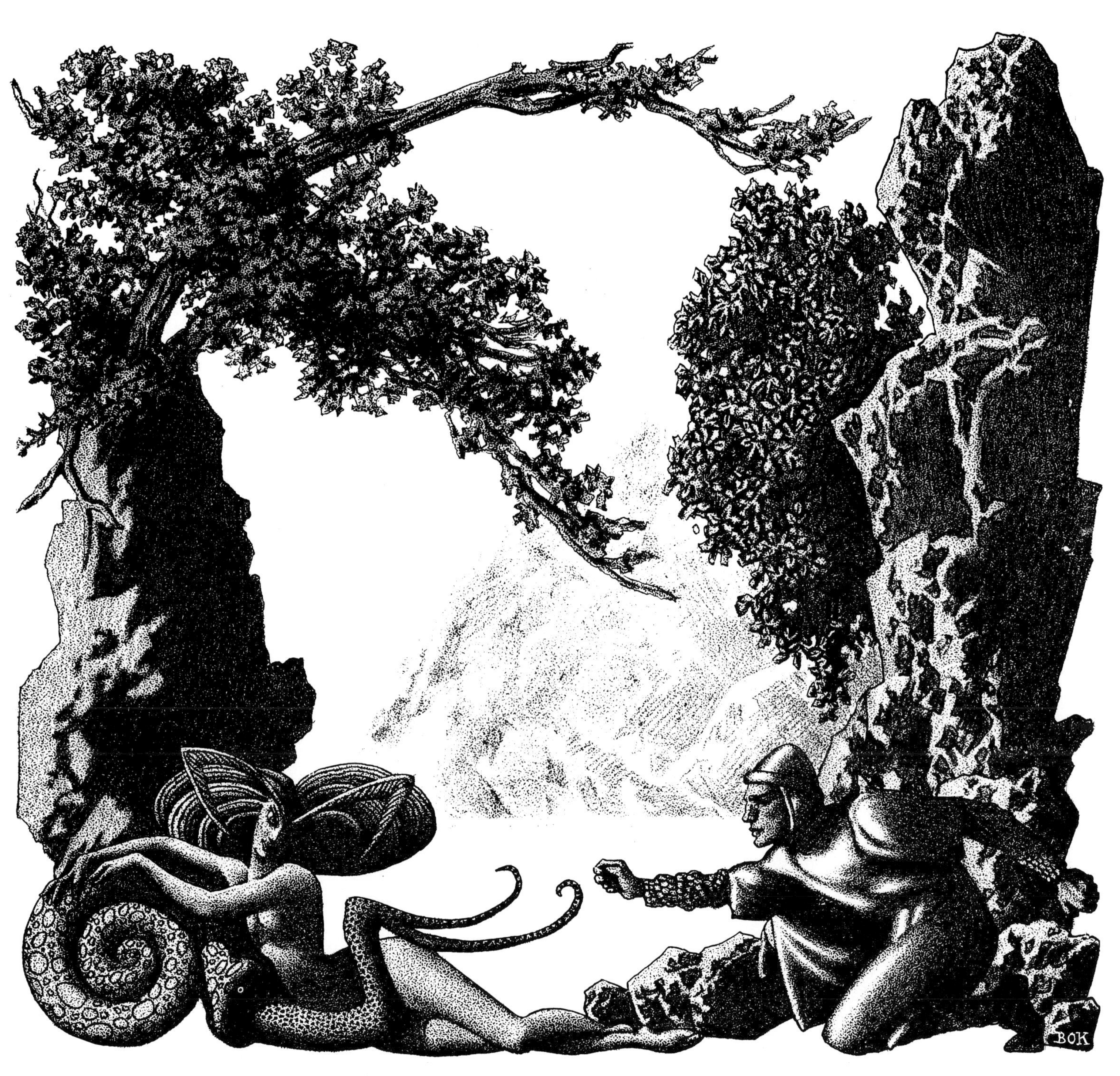

Illustration for "Haunted Hour" by Leah Bodine Drake, 1941.

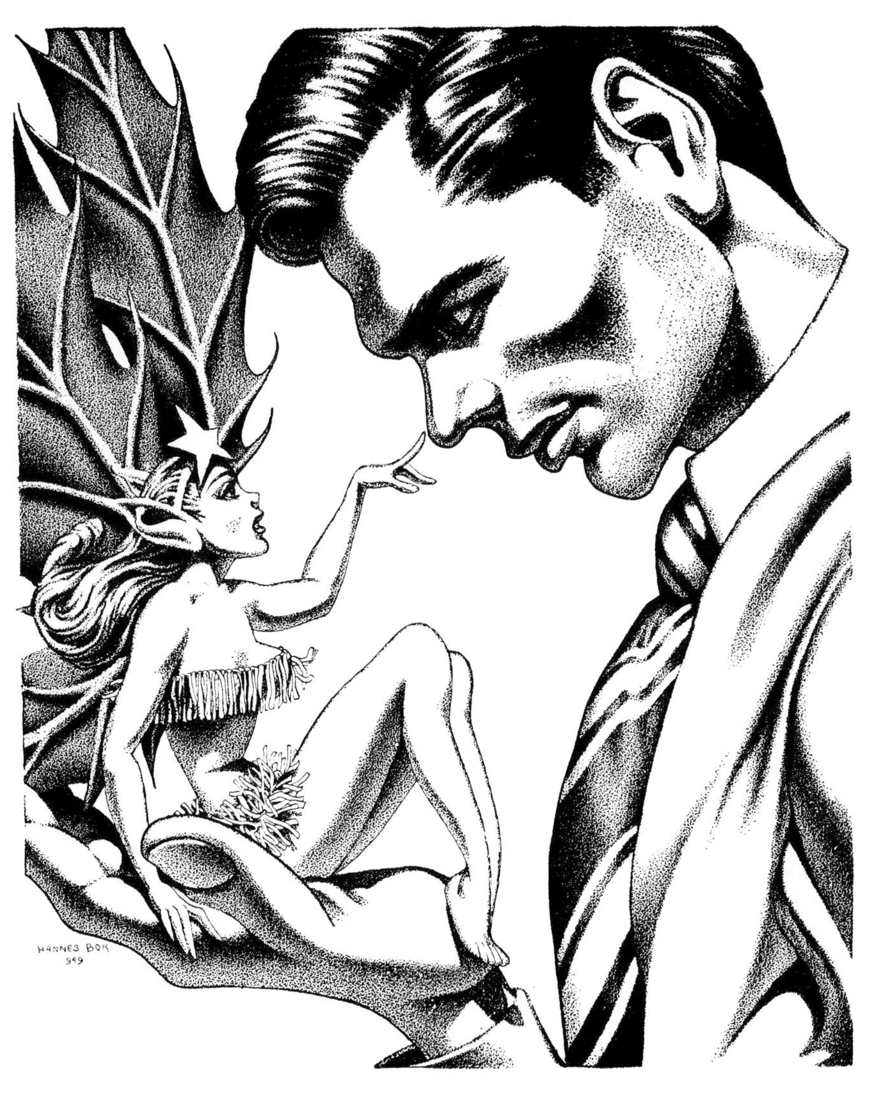

Illustration for "Winner Takes All" by William F. Temple, 1950.

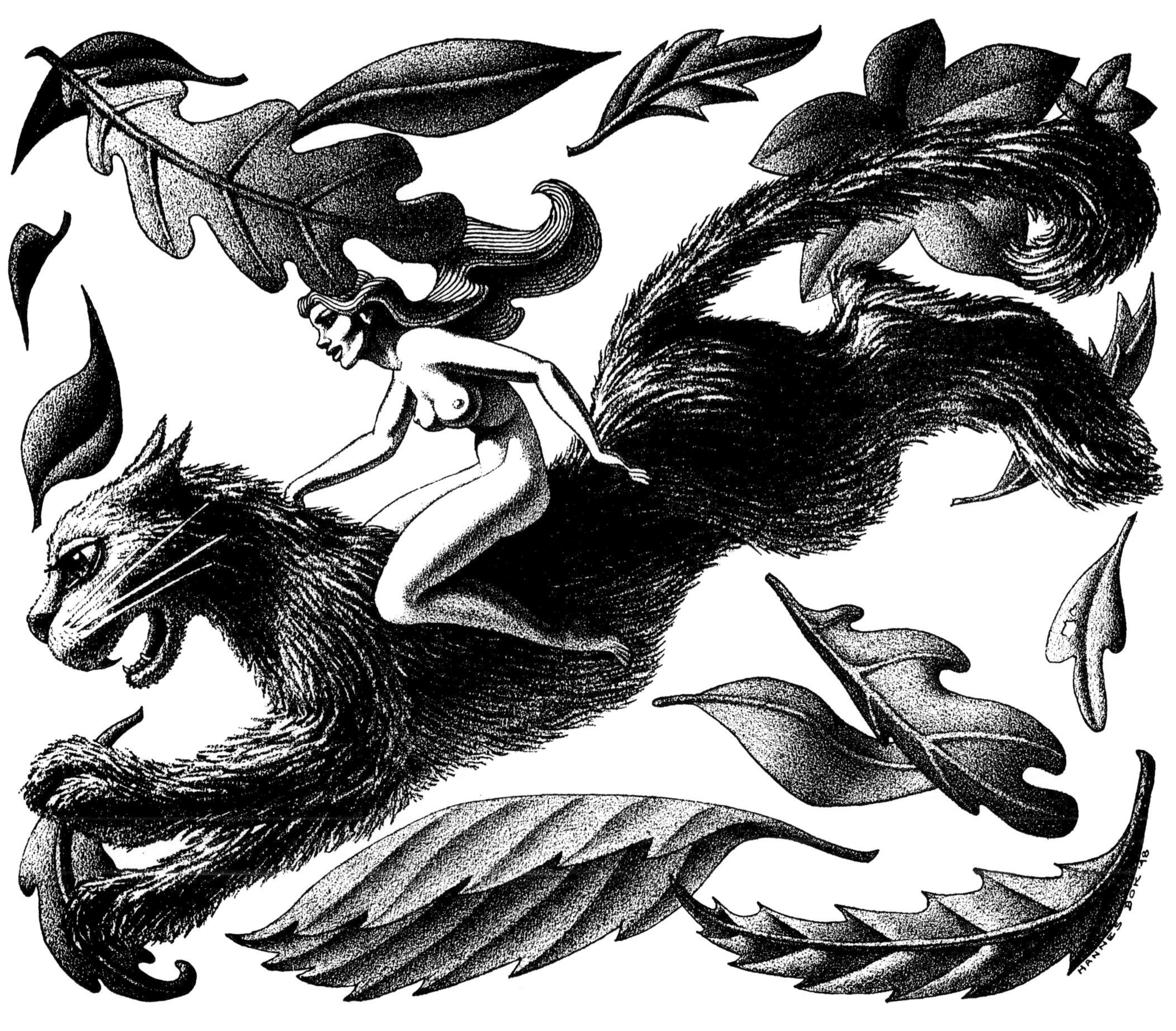

Illustration for "Halloween Ride," 1948.

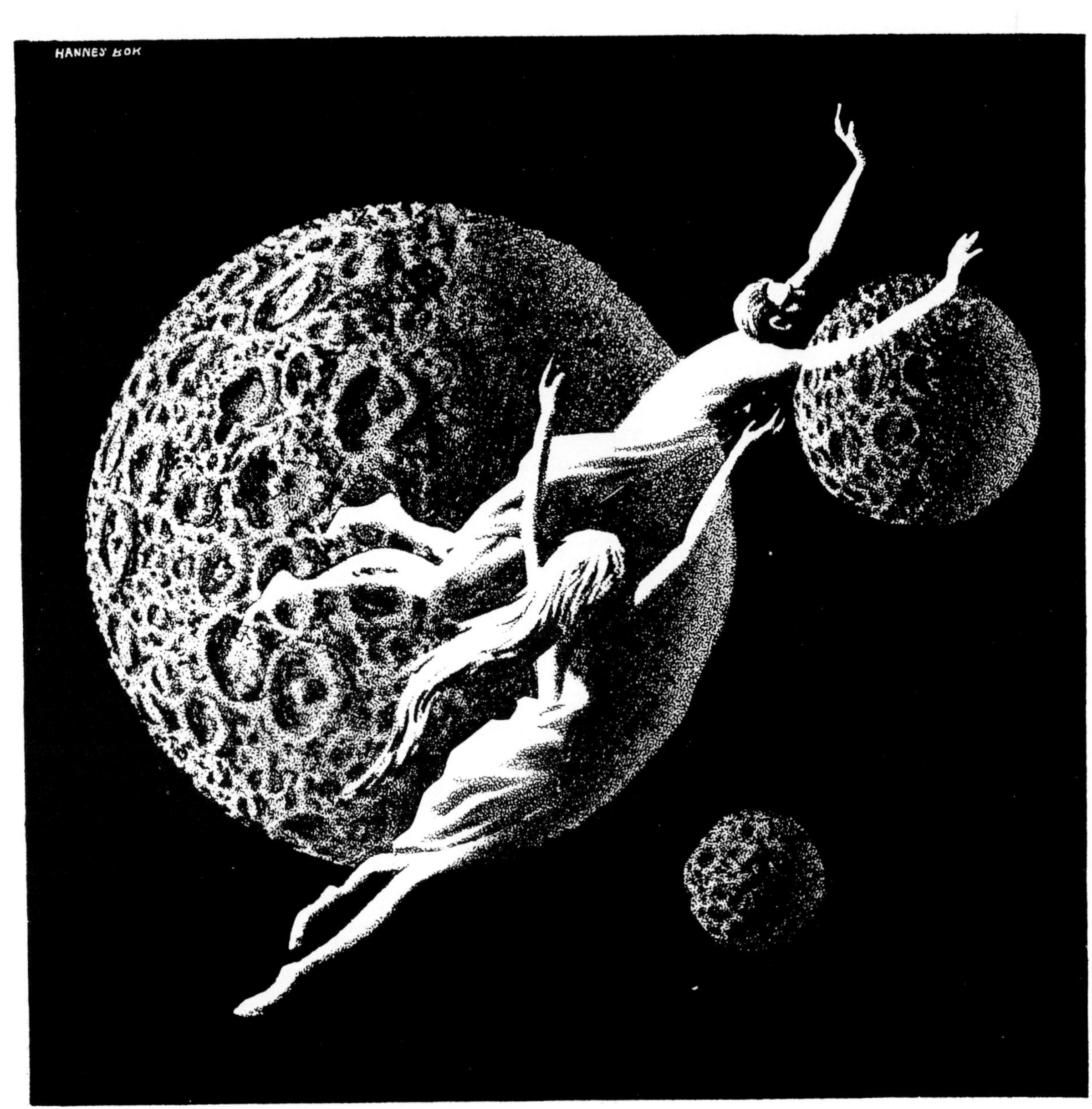

Illustration for "Voice in the Void" by Walter Kubilius, 1942.

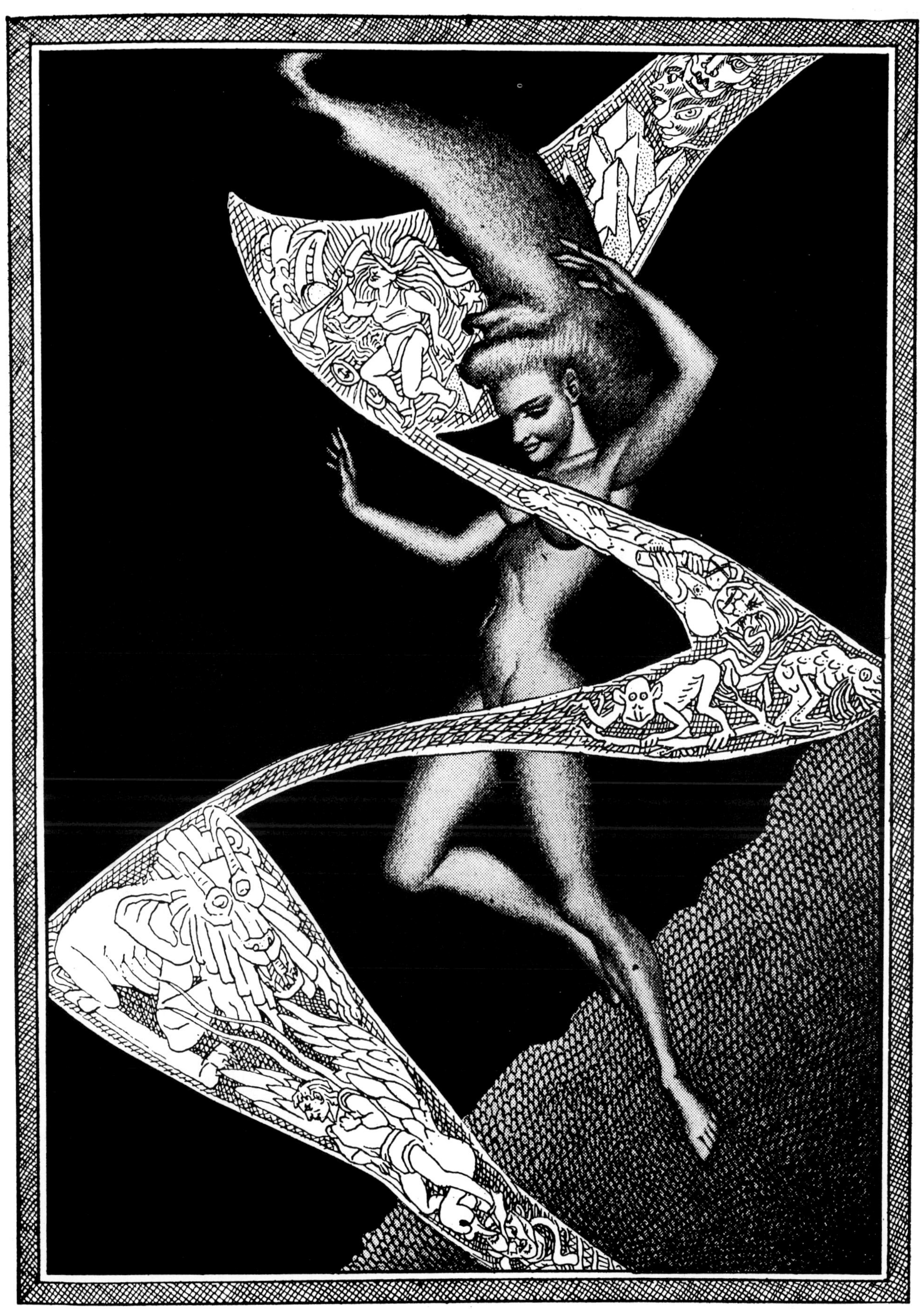

Illustration for "The Golden Road" by Cecil Corwin (C. M. Kornbluth), 1942.

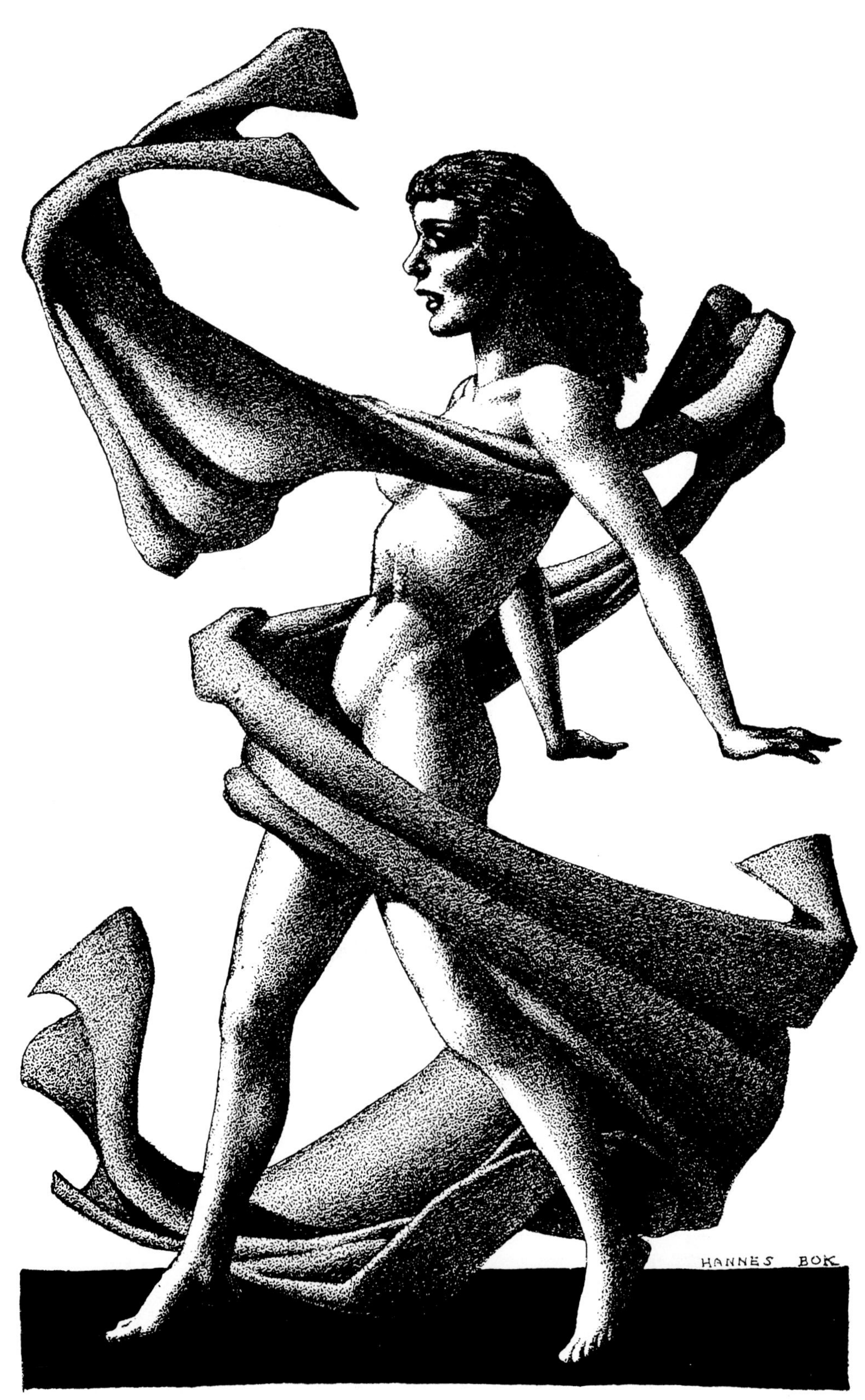

Illustration for "The Deadly Theory" by Greye La Spina, 1942.